Vocabulary Activities

Cambridge Handbooks for Language Teachers

This series, now with over 40 titles, offers practical ideas, techniques and activities for the teaching of English and other languages providing inspiration for both teachers and trainers.

Recent titles in this series:

Vocabulary Activities

Penny Ur

Consultant and editor: Scott Thornbury

CAMBRIDGE
UNIVERSITY PRESS

CAMBRIDGE
UNIVERSITY PRESS

University Printing House, Cambridge CB2 8BS, United Kingdom

One Liberty Plaza, 20th Floor, New York, NY 10006, USA

477 Williamstown Road, Port Melbourne, VIC 3207, Australia

4843/24, 2nd Floor, Ansari Road, Daryaganj, Delhi – 110002, India

79 Anson Road, #06–04/06, Singapore 079906

Cambridge University Press is part of the University of Cambridge.

It furthers the University's mission by disseminating knowledge in the pursuit of
education, learning and research at the highest international levels of excellence.

www.cambridge.org
Information on this title: www.cambridge.org/9780521181143

First published 2012
Reprinted 2017

Printed in Italy by Rotolito Lombarda S.p.A.

A catalogue record for this publication is available from the British Library

Library of Congress Cataloguing in Publication data
Ur, Penny.
Vocabulary activities / Penny Ur ; consultant and editor: Scott Thornbury.
    p. cm.
Includes bibliographical references and index.
ISBN 978-0-521-18114-3 (pbk. with cd-rom)
1. Vocabulary--Problems and exercises. 2. English language--Textbooks for foreign speakers. 3. English
language--Spoken English. 4. English language--Sound recordings for foreign speakers. I. Thornbury, Scott,
1950- II. Title.

PE1449.U7 2012.
428.2'4071--dc23

ISBN 978-0-521-18114-3 Paperback and CD-ROM

Contents

Thanks and acknowledgements

I would like to thank Scott Thornbury, the Series Editor, for insightful criticisms and some helpful additions to the first draft; and Verity Cole, at CreatEd, for her punctilious checking of format and style, and a number of gratefully accepted suggestions for improvement of the content.

My thanks also to Paul Nation and Norbert Schmitt for the knowledge of background theory and research on vocabulary teaching which I have gained through study of their books and articles; and particularly to Diane Schmitt, who generously made available to me sources and insights from research, as well as her own presentations and writing.

And a special debt of gratitude to Batia Laufer, my colleague at Haifa University and a renowned expert on vocabulary learning and teaching for sharing her expertise and knowledge through her published works, face-to-face meetings and email correspondence.

Introduction

Some years ago I wrote a book called *Grammar Practice Activities*. I
wrote it because, like many other language teachers, I was aware of the
importance of teaching grammar, but frustrated by the lack of interesting
and communicative grammar activities in my coursebooks. The book was
well-received, frequently reprinted, and more recently updated in a new
edition.[1] But grammar is, though perhaps the most written-about aspect
of language teaching and learning, by no means the most important. That
place is reserved for its **vocabulary**, which is the main carrier of meanings.
As David Wilkins puts it: 'While without grammar little can be conveyed,
without vocabulary nothing can be conveyed.'[2] As with grammar, interesting
and learning-rich activities are needed to help learners acquire, practise
and deepen their knowledge of the lexical items of a language. And as with
grammar, it seemed to me that teachers would be glad of a resource offering
a variety of such activities to supplement the material provided by their
coursebooks: hence *Vocabulary Activities*.

The book provides a varied set of vocabulary activities, most of which can
be used with whatever vocabulary items you are currently teaching: ones
that have come up in a text, for example, or ones connected to a theme or
topic you wish to engage with in the classroom. Most of the activities are
therefore 'generic' rather than limited to a particular set of items. So where
there are sample texts or lists of items in a *Box*, these usually function as
examples and illustrations.

The activities are varied also in the kinds of classes or student populations
they address: for ages ranging from young children to adults, and levels from
beginner to advanced. Many can be adapted for use with a range of different
kinds of classes.

The first section is headed *Guidelines* and provides some useful
background information and practical tips relating to the teaching of
vocabulary in general and the design and use of the activities in this book

---

[1] Ur, P. (2009). *Grammar Practice Activities*, Second Edition. Cambridge: Cambridge University
Press.
[2] Wilkins, D.A. (1972). *Linguistics in Language Teaching*. Massachusetts: MIT Press.

in particular. The second and major section, *Activities*, consists of the vocabulary activities themselves, organized under the headings: *Vocabulary expansion*; *Vocabulary review*; *Advanced vocabulary study*; *Vocabulary testing*; *Mainly for fun.*

Guidelines

BACKGROUND

What is *vocabulary*?

The simplest definition of vocabulary is 'the words of the language': but this is an oversimplification.

First, vocabulary does not just mean single words, but includes also *lexical chunks*, or *chunks* for short. These are groups of two or more words that convey a meaning in the same way a word does, and are learnt and retained in the memory as a single lexical unit.

Chunks may be short combinations like phrasal verbs (*look up*) or collocations, (words that tend to occur together: *to wage + war*), whole phrases (*in any case, once and for all*) or full sentences (*What's the matter? Let's call it a day*). Hence writers on vocabulary teaching tend to use the more comprehensive term *lexical items* rather than *words*.

Second, the term as it is used in this book excludes words that are *grammatical items*: words like *the, is, that, what, something*; pronouns, prepositions, numbers, basic auxiliary verbs like *do*, and so on. Grammatical items carry little or no meaning in themselves: they are, rather, the words used to connect lexical items – nouns, full verbs, adjectives, adverbs – with one another in order to create meaningful phrases or sentences (for ideas to teach such items, see *Grammar Practice Activities*). Grammatical items are closed sets, not open to expansion: nobody is about to add a new pronoun, for example, or a new definite article. Lexical items, in contrast, are an open set, constantly being added to (and lost, as archaic words gradually go out of use).

Why is vocabulary important, and how much do learners need to know?

Learning the vocabulary of a language is important simply because it is mainly the vocabulary which carries meanings. You can usually convey what you want to say through vocabulary alone, with minimal grammar – but not the other way around. Newspaper headings often omit most of the grammar and still convey their message: for example, 'London Rail Accident'. Moreover, it has been shown that in reading comprehension you cannot be sure of accurately grasping the main messages of a text without knowing in advance between 95% and 98% of its words, and that you need to know about 8,000 words in order to be able to understand an unsimplified written text in English.[3] This means that schoolchildren learning English as an additional language who want to achieve this level of knowledge – and who typically study it for eight years for an average of 30 weeks a year – need to learn about 30 new items a week on average, even without taking into account the reviewing needed for thorough mastery. If the aim is to learn only basic conversational English, of course, then the number will be much smaller; but if it is advanced Academic English, then it will be larger.

What needs to be learnt about a lexical item?

Spoken and written forms, meaning

We begin by teaching what the word sounds and looks like and what it means. The spoken form and meaning are usually taught before the written form. In some cases – a course aimed at oral communication, for example – you might not even bother about teaching how to spell the item at all. Also it is worth noting that the *receptive* aspects are taught before the *productive*: students need to know how to recognize and understand spoken and written versions before they can actually produce them themselves. But eventually both spoken and written forms as well as meaning need to be learnt, both receptively and productively, and all of these are dealt with in most of the activities in this book. Other aspects discussed below, such as *grammar, morphology, collocation, connotation, register, appropriateness* and *semantic links* with other items are usually taught and learnt later.

Grammar

Apart from generalized grammatical rules, many lexical words have their own particular grammatical forms and different ways they link syntactically with other items in sentences. These need to be learnt as part of the knowledge of the word itself. Examples are the irregular plurals of nouns like *man, woman, child*; simple past forms of verbs like *know, say, go*; the fact that the verb *enjoy* is followed by the *-ing* form of the verb and the adjective *frightened* by the preposition *of*.

[3] Schmitt, N. (2008). Instructed second language vocabulary learning. *Language Teaching Research, 12*(3), 329–363.

Morphology

Morphology refers to the way words are constructed from *morphemes* or basic word components. If you know the meanings of the morphemes of a compound word you can usually work out what the full word means: for example, *bathroom* (*bath* + *room*) or *bookshop* (*book* + *shop*). And if you know one member of a word family (for example, *product*), you can often understand or work out the others (*production, productive, unproductive*). A set of morphemes which are particularly useful to know are the prefixes (for example, *pre-, un-, auto-, super-*) and suffixes (for example, *-ible, -ly, -ify, -tion*), as well as the meanings of some basic Latin or Greek roots. (For prefixes and suffixes see *1.4.1 Suffixes for parts of speech* and *1.4.2 Exploring affixes*; for Latin or Greek roots see *1.4.5 From Greek and Latin (1)* and *1.4.6 From Greek and Latin (2)*) .

Collocation

Collocation refers to the way particular words tend to occur together with other particular words in sentences. Learners need to know what other words a specific item tends to *collocate* with in phrases or sentences. For example, the word *tall* tends to collocate with people, trees or buildings, whereas *high* collocates with mountains or abstract nouns like *price, profile*. Some 'strong' collocations are in fact *chunks*, lexical items in themselves (*blind date*, for example). Others are 'weaker': they represent the preferences, as it were, that single words have as to which other words they tend to come before or after (like *work + hard*). (See *1.3.1 What usually goes with this word?(1)* for an example of an activity that focuses on collocations.)

Connotation

The dictionary definition of a word is its main meaning or *denotation*. *Connotation*, in contrast, refers to the underlying associations of the word, usually positive or negative. For example, the two words *damp* and *moist* have similar denotations: they mean 'slightly wet'. Their connotations, however, are quite different: *damp* has negative connotations, and *moist* positive : if your clothes have not dried yet after washing you might call them *damp*, whereas your freshly baked cake would be soft and *moist*. The same words may have different connotations in different cultures: in the UK, for example, the word *dog* can often have positive connotations of faithfulness and friendliness, whereas in the Middle East it has negative ones of dirt and inferiority (see *3.2.1 It doesn't mean quite the same thing (1)*).

Appropriateness

Some items are appropriate for use in some contexts and not others. One major distinction is between formal and informal use: a word like *guys*, meaning 'people', for example, is appropriate for informal conversation, but not for formal speech or writing. Other aspects of appropriateness have to do with choice of words to express identity or culture. *Slang or jargon* items are used in specific contexts, sometimes by particular communities, and may not be appropriate elsewhere. Some terms are actually offensive if used inappropriately. Most of the vocabulary your students learn will in fact be stylistically neutral – you can use it in any context – but those which are clearly appropriate for particular contexts need to be taught as such (see, for example, 3.2.9 *Is it appropriate?*).

Semantic links with other items

It is sometimes helpful also to work on links with other words. These links may be any of the following: *antonyms* (*large* → *small*), *synonyms* (*large* → *big*), *superordinates* and *hyponyms* (*furniture* → *chair*, *table*), *associates*, or words from the same *semantic set* (*nose, eyes, mouth, ears*). It may be useful to exploit semantic links in practising or testing new items (see, for example, 2.1.12 *Sort them out (1)*, and 4.1.4 *Multiple matching*), though there is some evidence to suggest that presenting new items within such groups or pairs may not be such a good idea (see the question on this in the *FAQs* below).

Vocabulary teaching

People learning their own mother tongue acquire its vocabulary mainly through interaction with those around them, and through reading and listening. They have opportunities to interact with other native speakers for a large part of their waking hours every day, and plenty of time during childhood and adolescence to read an enormous quantity of text, either print or digital, and to listen to a lot of spoken language. This is not true of most learners of an additional language in formal courses of study, whose encounter with the target language may begin only when they enter school, or later, and is typically limited to three or four hours a week. Such a situation does not provide the sheer quantity of exposure to the target language, spoken or written, that is needed in order to 'pick up' large amounts of vocabulary in the same sort of natural way that native speakers do.

The fact that learners of an additional language in formal courses get only a relatively limited amount of exposure to the target language would explain why, as research has shown,[4] extensive reading is not enough: it cannot, on its own, provide a satisfactory basis for learning of the wide vocabulary needed by such students. An optimally effective programme has to include also deliberate, focused teaching of lexical items.

One of the reasons for the necessity for a substantial component of vocabulary teaching in the classroom is the fact that you do not normally learn a new item through one encounter with it: you need to re-encounter it several times (probably between six and sixteen[5]) in order to remember it – and your second encounter needs to take place before you've forgotten the first! For the basic, frequent items, this is not a problem: you are likely to come across a common word like *go* plenty of times in everyday conversation and reading. But once you get beyond the first few hundred most common words this cannot be taken for granted. Take a word like *kitchen* for example: after we have taught this for the first time in a text from our coursebook, how often is it likely to recur by chance in interactive communication or new texts in the four-lessons-a-week learning situation? Probably not enough. And the problem of providing for such re-encounters gets more and more acute as the students' level rises and new items become less and less commonly used. Which is why we need to provide systematic and cumulative vocabulary review activities in the classroom (see activities suggested in 2 *Vocabulary review*).

Vocabulary assessment
We sometimes need to assess how much vocabulary our students know, which is normally done through vocabulary tests, like those shown in 4 *Vocabulary testing*.

Summative and formative assessment
Assessment may be *summative* or *formative*. Summative assessment is done to show how good students' vocabulary knowledge is: in general, or at the end of a particular course. It is expressed in a grade only: as a percentage, for example, or a letter (*A, B, C*). The purpose of formative assessment, in

---

[4] Laufer, B. (2003). Vocabulary acquisition in a second language: do learners really acquire most vocabulary by reading? Some empirical evidence. *Canadian Modern Language Review*, 59(4), 567–587.

[5] Zahar, R., Cobb, T. & Spada, N. (2001). Acquiring vocabulary through reading: effects of frequency and contextual richness. *Canadian Modern Language Review* , 57(4), 544–72.

contrast, is to inform further learning and teaching: to make both teachers and students aware of how good the students' knowledge is and what their exact strengths and weaknesses are (*diagnostic assessment*). So formative assessment is normally accompanied by *corrective feedback* (see the *Practical Tip* on this below), whereas summative assessment is not. Self-assessment is particularly useful for formative purposes: students can assess their own vocabulary knowledge if the correct answers to a test are made available to them, or if they use a web tool such as *Lextutor*'s self-test (http://www.lextutor.ca/tests/).

Specific and general vocabulary knowledge

Vocabulary tests usually relate to a specific set of items learnt during the period preceding the test; and this is the main purpose of most of the testing procedures suggested in *4 Vocabulary testing*. But occasionally we may want to test students' overall knowledge, in which case we might use procedures such as *4.1.15 Lexical frequency profile*.

Validity and reliability

You need to make sure that your tests are *valid*. In the case of vocabulary assessment, this means that they test both receptive and productive knowledge, and a reasonable range of aspects of vocabulary knowledge. So a vocabulary test should not be limited to one type of test item, but combine several of the types described in *4 Vocabulary testing*. Tests also need to be *reliable* – producing consistent results – so make sure that the criteria for checking are clear enough so that if the test is done again with the same class or another class, or checked by another teacher, its results will be able to be reliably compared with the previous ones.

Testing versus reviewing

There is a significant difference between activities such as those shown in *1 Vocabulary expansion* and *2 Vocabulary review*, and the tests described in *4 Vocabulary testing*. This is not so much in the actual procedure itself – some procedures, such as cloze, may be used for either – but in the way it is presented, administered and responded to. Essentially, activities that review vocabulary aim to consolidate and deepen learners' incipient knowledge; in other words, their aim is to teach. Activities that test aim to find out what students know; they may not result in much learning.

A review activity is typically preceded by some kind of preparation or review, refreshing students' memory of the target items. The class then does a task which gets them to engage with these items in interesting and meaningful ways in order to deepen their awareness of the different ways the items can be used, and to reinforce their knowledge, so that they will be able to retrieve and use these items next time more quickly, appropriately and fluently. A test activity does not prepare the students before the procedure, but simply gives them tasks which demand recognition or production of a set of vocabulary items in order to find out if they know them or not.

The aim of a review activity is the production of lots of successful, fluent vocabulary use. So there is plenty of room for peer teaching and collaboration, for creative and original responses. But there is no particular need for assessment or the giving of grades. It is the process of doing the task, not the product, which is important. A test is the reverse: the quantity of responses is not important, but whether they are correct or not; there is no room for peer collaboration; creative or original responses are less welcome because they are more difficult to assess. It is the product which is important, and, of course, the assessment and grade.

Vocabulary teaching in practice: Some FAQs

How do I select which vocabulary items to teach?

In general, it's most important to teach the most frequent and useful items first, so that learners are enabled to understand and convey simple messages. Even at higher levels, frequency and usefulness remain the main criteria for selection.

You can find out which the most common items are in English used for a variety of communicative purposes by looking at frequency lists now easily accessible on the Internet (see, for example, http://www.lextutor.ca/freq/lists_download/). Note that if you are teaching English for Specific Purposes (Business English, for example), then obviously the items you will define as 'frequent' or 'useful' may differ substantially from those provided by such sources.

There are, however, reasons why you might want to select occasional words or expressions that are not particularly frequent: because they are useful for classroom interaction, because they are easily taught and learnt (*cognates*, for instance), because they are relevant to students' own lives or surroundings, because they are interesting, or because they are the basis for lots of useful derivatives (for example *use → useful, useless, usable ...*).

Do I have to teach all the words in a coursebook text?
Not necessarily. For one thing, the text often includes items which, for beginner or intermediate classes, are not very useful to teach for permanent acquisition (too difficult and too rare to be useful to students). For another, the compiler of the vocabulary list does not know your class, and may not include items that may be relevant to their own context, and which they need to know. Finally, coursebook vocabulary lists tend to focus on single words, and often omit useful chunks and collocations; though a number of more recently published materials[6] are based on corpus data and focus far more on *multi-word expressions* than did the older ones.

So it's important to search through the text for new vocabulary yourself and not to rely only on the coursebook's selection. Your own intuitions about which items your students are likely to find useful in the future are pretty reliable, so write down all the items you think need active teaching and review. You'll find there are also several items that students need to understand for the particular context of the text in question, but are unlikely to need so much for their own use later: these you need to explain for immediate comprehension but don't necessarily have to review and test.

A useful tool is *VocabProfile* in *The Compleat Lexical Tutor* http://www.lextutor.ca/vp/bnc/. Paste your text into the box provided, and then click on *submit*. The next page will show you how commonly used the words in the text are. The words are divided into different lists: ones that occur in the top thousand most frequent words, ones that occur in the second thousand most frequent, and so on. So you can make sure that you teach or review the most common ones. The problem is that this website does not distinguish between *homographs* (for example, *bat* used in a game and *bat* the animal), or parts of speech (*a bridge* vs *to bridge*), and does not identify lexical chunks: so you'll need to add these from your own study of the text.

What items might I teach other than those that appear in the coursebook?
You'll find that you are occasionally teaching items that 'happen to come up': a student has come across a word and wants you to explain it; there has been something interesting on the news that provides new lexis; you find yourself using a new item as you speak, and need to make sure it's understood. Just

---

[6] For example, Clementson, C., Tilbury, A., Hendra, LA., Rea, D., Doff, A. & Goldstein, B. (2010). *English Unlimited*. Cambridge: Cambridge University Press.

make sure that you note down these items for later review, or they'll get lost and forgotten.

One important additional area of basic lexis to teach is classroom language: the kind of words and expressions teachers and students might need to use during a lesson. Particularly for beginner or younger students, it's worth spending time at the beginning of a course helping them to get used to understanding and using such items. (See *1.1.1 Classroom language* for some useful core items.)

How many new words should I teach in a lesson?

This depends, of course, on the level and age of your students. But about ten or twelve new items a lesson is a reasonable estimate to start with, in order to provide sufficient time for dealing with both meaning and form, and for initial practice. (This number needs to be lowered, of course, with less advanced or younger students, and raised with older and more academic ones.) Which means about 30–40 new items a week, or an average of nearly a thousand a year. Note that this relates only to new items; you will need to devote quite a lot of time to cumulative review of previously learnt material.

Can you give me a few ideas for presenting new vocabulary?

The main problem here is how to present the meaning; but remember that the form of the new item is just as important as the meaning: it's no use knowing a meaning if you don't know what the corresponding item sounds or looks like! As you teach the meanings, say the new item several times, and get students to repeat it; make sure it is written up on the board, possibly together with its phonemic transcript, and that students also write it down themselves.

There are lots of ways of presenting meanings. At beginner or elementary level, where the meanings of new vocabulary tend to be more concrete, you can use pictures,[7] realia (actual objects or toy models), gesture and mime. Later, you are more likely to use translation, definition, give examples or hints and provide sample sentences or phrases in context. Probably the most effective for classes who share a mother tongue known to the teacher is translation, for various reasons (see the question on this below).

---

[7] For some good ways to use pictures, see Goldstein, B. (2008). *Working with Images.* Cambridge: Cambridge University Press.

Sending the learners to a dictionary is less efficient. First, it's very time-consuming: more time is spent turning pages, or finding the dictionary website and typing in the item to be found, than is spent reading the definition. Second, the dictionary often provides a number of meanings, so the learner has to look through them all to find the one they want – and risks choosing the wrong one. Learners will have plenty of opportunities to use the dictionary when a teacher is not available; it doesn't make sense to send them to the dictionary when you are there to help.

So you think dictionaries shouldn't be used in the classroom?

No, just that they're not a very efficient way of presenting meanings of new items in the classroom. Obviously the dictionary is a valuable tool for the learner working individually to expand their own vocabulary. So it makes sense to do some focused dictionary work in the classroom in order to help them make good use of it when they are on their own.

Beyond this, the dictionary can, and should, be used in the classroom to expand and enrich knowledge of items students have already encountered: to check pronunciation and spelling, to look for other possible meanings (see *1.2.11 What other meanings does it have?*), to learn collocations and idioms the item is used in (see *1.3.1 What usually goes with this word?(1)*), even their etymology (see *3.2.13 All you know about a word*).[8] It's just the first-time learning of meaning of a new item that I feel is best mediated by the teacher, if present, rather than by the dictionary.

Is it a good idea to teach items in semantic sets, like colours?

Probably not, at least at first encounter. Research[9] indicates that students learn better when items are unrelated, or related only as they naturally co-occur in context. In other words, it's better to teach *blue* for the first time together with *sky* or *dark* and not *blue* together with *red, yellow, green*. The trouble is that a lot of beginner coursebooks, as well as vocabulary courses, tend to teach new words in lexical sets, as they are so convenient to collect and present. But teaching convenience is not the same as teaching/learning effectiveness. The problem is, apparently, that if you teach lots of words that mean 'the same kind of thing', learners get confused between

---

[8] For some useful and imaginative ways to use the dictionary, see Leaney, C. (2007). *Dictionary Activities*. Cambridge: Cambridge University Press.

[9] Papathanasiou, E. (2009). An investigation of two ways of presenting vocabulary. *ELT Journal*, 63(4), 313–322.

them. In the same way, it's probably not a good idea to present new items in groupings such as *synonyms* (*big/large/great*), *antonyms* (*fast/slow*), *homonyms* (*bear/bear*), *homophones* (*accept/except*) or *homographs* (*lead* [led]/*lead* [liːd]).

Having said that, it **is** a useful strategy to use such groupings for vocabulary expansion (see for example *1.2.6 Does it have an opposite?*) or review activities (see for example *2.1.15 Flexible odd one out*). If the students already have some knowledge of a number of items, learnt initially within their own individual contexts, they can then use these as a basis to add further similar vocabulary. Similarly, such items can be effectively reviewed and consolidated through work on categorization, ordering etc., using higher-order thinking skills (see for example *2.1.14 Arrange along a continuum*).

What are some good vocabulary-learning strategies I can teach my students?

This is a really important point. You can teach only a limited amount of vocabulary in the classroom; beyond that the students need to learn on their own, and the more initiative they take in identifying, noticing, learning and reviewing new vocabulary, the better. Here are some ideas you can recommend to them:

- **Look for new words.** Keep an eye out for new words or expressions that you come across in books, on the Internet, on notices or advertisements. Make a mental note, and then look them up or ask someone what they mean at the first opportunity.
- **Don't be afraid to ask.** If you don't understand something, ask someone who knows the language better than you do. People are usually happy to help!
- **Keep a vocabulary notebook (paper or digital).** Write down new items as you learn them, with the L1 equivalent. You can tick them off or delete them when you're sure you know them. Keep the notebook in your pocket or bag, so that when you come across new items during the day you can pull it out and jot down the new item immediately.
- **Make small cards, or slips of paper.** Write new words or expressions on one side and the L1 translation on the other. Keep them in a plastic bag or box in your pocket or bag, and take them out when you are waiting around or travelling by public transport, go through them and remind yourself. Throw away the ones you are sure you know. Such cards can also be used for review in class.

- **Connect keywords with words in your language.** When learning a new word, try to find a word or name in your own language that sounds similar and invent a reason to connect the two. For example, if you're an English speaker learning the French word *arbre* (*tree*), you might connect it with the word 'Arab' and imagine an Arab sitting under a tree. This works as a mnemonic, helping you to recall the new word when needed.
- **Spend ten minutes a day.** Take ten minutes every day to go over new vocabulary you've learnt, whether in your notebook, on card, or in the textbook.
- **Use bilingual dictionaries.** Use a bilingual rather than monolingual dictionary to look up a word for the first time: it's faster and easier to use, and just as accurate. Use a monolingual dictionary for further explanations and examples.
- **Use digital dictionaries.** Install an online dictionary on the 'favorites/ bookmarks' on your internet browser, or on your mobile phone or tablet, so you can look up things quickly and easily: The *Cambridge Dictionary Online*, for example (http://www.dictionary.cambridge.org/). There are also commercial programs (*Babylon*, for example (see http:// www.babylon.com)) which enable you just to click on an unknown word and get a translation or dictionary definition.
- **Use the dictionary while you're reading (paper or digital).** Check out the meanings of occasional new words and write them down. Not all of them, of course: if you stop to look up every single word you don't know, then you won't enjoy the reading or improve your reading fluency. But do so every now and then.

Is it a good idea to give students lists of vocabulary items to learn?
Yes; like many 'old-fashioned' ideas, this one has proved itself a useful procedure in practice.[10] 'Learn these words, I'll test you on Monday' is a perfectly legitimate and learning-rich procedure. But there are a couple of reservations that need to be made here:

- First, learning lists of items contributes to good learning, but does not on its own ensure permanent remembering: you're going to need to review the items later in other ways.

---

[10] See, for example, Laufer, B., & Shmueli, K. (1997). Memorizing new words: does teaching have anything to do with it? *RELC Journal, 28*(1), 89–108.

- Second, learning lists is a bit boring. It needs to be supplemented by more imaginative and interesting activities, such as those suggested later in this book.
- Third, lists, of course, do not provide opportunities for engaging with the vocabulary within a wider context: sentences, texts, interactions. So that's another reason to supplement with other kinds of activities.

Can I use translation when teaching vocabulary?

Yes. Not just 'can' but rather 'should', if you have a monolingual class whose language you know. To present the meanings of new words, translation is at least as accurate as other ways of explaining meanings, and much quicker. It saves time which can then be used for supplementing the translated meaning with English definitions and examples and for engaging with the new item in English contexts.

Translation is also a useful means of testing students' knowledge of the basic form and meaning of new items: if they can translate a mother-tongue item into English, or vice versa, that's a good indication that they know it.

It is also something that students feel comfortable doing: they are confident in their own language, which thus provides a firm and reliable basis for venturing into the L2. And many intermediate or advanced students enjoy the exercise of looking for appropriate equivalents, whether from L1 to L2 or the reverse (see, for example, *3.2.5 What's the best way to translate . . . ?*).

Can you suggest some ideas for quick vocabulary review?

Here are a few:

- Just write up the items on the board; ask students if there are any whose meaning they **don't** remember, and tell them.
- Give students five minutes during class time to look through their notebooks or vocabulary cards and review recently learnt items.
- Dictate the items in L1, ask students to say the English equivalents; or vice versa.
- Ask each student to say one word or expression they've recently learnt, round the class. (It's often not necessary even to demand the meaning: the fact that they've remembered it is a good indication that they also know what it means – we rarely remember meaningless noises!)
- See *2 Vocabulary review* for some more ideas, many of which can be got through fairly quickly.

Isn't it more important for students to understand items than produce them?
Yes, receptive knowledge is indeed more important than productive: learners – indeed most of us, even in our mother tongue – are likely to spend far more time reading and listening than writing or speaking. And the number of words you can understand is always more than the number you produce and use yourself. But on the other hand it has been shown that the use of practice that includes *output* (production) results in better learning.[11] So even if you don't expect your learners to master items to the extent of being able to use them fluently in their own production, activities that get them to produce them within limited contexts are important: these will ultimately deepen and broaden both receptive and productive knowledge.

How can I make vocabulary review activities more interesting?
There are various ways, some or all of which are implemented in the activities in this book:

- Make the task objective clear from the beginning, so students have a clear idea what they're meant to achieve. Often it's best to present this in the form of the actual outcome expected (a list, a picture, a decision).
- Design the task so that this outcome is meaningful (for example, a solution to a problem) rather than just for language display (for example, the answers to multiple-choice questions).
- Share frankly with students the pedagogical aim (what useful learning they'll get out of doing the activity).
- Use visual materials where possible: pictures, diagrams, something to read; students lose interest if they have nothing particular to look at.
- Design tasks to be open ended (lots of possible right answers) rather than closed ended (one right answer). Open-ended tasks produce unpredictable, often original or funny, answers that keep students interested. (See, for example, the open-ended cues in *1.2.1 How many more can you think of?*)
- Use game-like strategies, like introducing limiting 'rules' ('you can't use the letter *B*', 'you have to do this within two minutes', 'you have to try to remember the words without peeping'), or group competition.
- Use higher-order thinking skills, like prioritizing, or distinguishing between true and false or fact and opinion, or comparing and contrasting, rather than just recall or basic comprehension.

[11] Laufer, B. (2005). Focus on form in second language vocabulary learning. *EUROSLA Yearbook*, 5, 223–250.

- Get students to apply the items to themselves in some way (*personalization*), involving their own experiences, tastes, opinions and aspirations.
- Make sure all, or as many as possible, students participate in the activity. So use the conventional teacher–student 'ping-pong' interaction as little as possible, go more for rapid brainstorming, pair- or group-work or individual work.

How should I correct vocabulary or spelling mistakes in written work?

There are three main possibilities here: just to underline the mistake; underline and add a code in the margin (*V* for wrong or inappropriate vocabulary item, *Sp* for spelling, *C* for a mistake in upper or lower case of letters); or write in the correct form. In general the research[12] indicates that writing in the correct form is the most helpful to students – though also the most time consuming! If the mistakes have occurred in written composition, students should be asked to rewrite the composition incorporating the correct forms, in order to reinforce the corrections.

How should I correct vocabulary or pronunciation mistakes in oral work?

The most common way is just to repeat the student's utterance with the correct pronunciation, or replacing their mistaken item with the correct one. This is called *recast* and it is very quick and easy: but for this very reason, students may not always pay attention and remember what you said! It is worth taking a moment or two of class time to draw attention to the acceptable form, perhaps explain what the mistake was and clarify any questions arising from the correction.

Using this book: some tips

Skim through it first.

- Don't try to read this book cover to cover: it's meant to be dipped into, used selectively. A first step is to leaf through, stopping to read any activity that catches your attention, getting to know the layout and the way the activities are presented.

---

[12] Chandler, J. (2003). The efficacy of various kinds of error feedback for improvement in the accuracy and fluency of L2 student writing. *Journal of Second Language Writing*, 12(3), 267–296.

- Note that the headings are usually fairly 'transparent', so if you read the heading of the activity and the brief note headed *Outline* under it, you'll have a fairly good idea of what it's about and whether it might be useful to you, without needing to read through the entire procedure.

Check out the initial rubrics before planning.

Under the headings are menu boxes, which provide preliminary useful information about the activity:

- **Outline:** summarizes the content and aims of the activity.
- **Focus:** provides information on the main teaching aim and focus.
- **Age:** relates to the recommended ages for which the activity is appropriate. These are roughly defined as follows:
  - Young: age 5–8
  - Pre-adolescent: age 9–12
  - Adolescent: age 13–17
  - Adult: age 18 upwards.
- **Level:** relates to the level, again roughly defined as follows:
  - Beginner: A1/A2 of the CEFR (*Common European Framework of Reference for Languages*)
  - Intermediate: B1/B2 of the CEFR
  - Advanced: C1/C2 of the CEFR.
- **Time:** suggests how much time the activity will probably take: but of course this will vary, sometimes widely, depending on the class and how the activity develops.
- **Preparation:** gives details on what you need to prepare ahead of time.

Where possible, use your own texts and vocabulary lists, not the ones in the *Boxes*.

Most of the activities in this book can be used with almost any set of vocabulary items or text. I've given some sample material in the *Boxes*, to provide illustrations, but you should, in most cases, be able to base the procedures on the material you are teaching in your classes. Some activities are, in fact, based on particular sets of vocabulary items and here I've tried to give as comprehensive lists as possible. Usually such lists are divided into two or three levels.

Don't feel you have to do it exactly the way it says.

The main function of this book is to give you ideas which you then adapt and change to fit your own needs. If you feel the way I've presented it is not appropriate for you, then change it in any way you like.

Check out the *Variations*.

If you really like a particular activity, check out the *Variations*, because these may offer an alternative approach which you might like to try, even the first time you do the activity. I wrote them separately, because I wanted to keep the basic *Procedure* as simple and clear as possible; but often they provide some good ideas you might want to use immediately.

Use the CD-ROM.

If you need to use lists, texts or illustrations from the *Boxes*, use the CD-ROM rather than copying from the book: it'll come out clearer, and the illustrations can be copied in colour.

Make notes in the margins!

I was told as a child never to write in a book; but that doesn't apply to this one! When you've used an activity, note beside it such things as:

- how it went in general: a ✓ or ✓✓ if it went well, a ✗ or ✗✗ if it went badly
- any problems that came up
- any suggestions for altering
- any suggestions for adding and omitting
- appropriateness or inappropriateness for a particular class
- further ideas on how to do it next time.

1   Vocabulary expansion

The activities in this section are designed to create opportunities for students to encounter new vocabulary. At this point the aim is for students to pay attention to the new items and to start learning them. But in order to remember them more permanently, they will need to do further review: either very short reminders (see the question on this in the *FAQs*), or full review activities, as suggested in 2 *Vocabulary review*.

In any case, students should be encouraged at the end of each activity to note down in their vocabulary notebooks the new items they have learnt, or make word cards from them (see the questions on vocabulary notebooks and word cards in the *FAQs*).

1.1 BUILDING ON THE INDIVIDUAL

These activities expand vocabulary by drawing on the teacher's or students' initiative based on individual knowledge, experience or needs as the source of the new items.

1.1.1 Classroom language

Outline	Students learn useful phrases for use in the classroom.
Focus	Teacher and textbook instructions, learner classroom requests
Age	Young–Adolescent
Level	Beginner
Time	Three or four minutes per lesson
Preparation	A set of useful classroom interactional utterances or texts, as shown in *Box 1.1.1*.

Procedure

1 Teach the students four or five of the *interactive items* in one of the first lessons you have with them, and make sure you review them later.
2 Continue to add to these in later lessons, and to review ones you have taught earlier. Then teach the *instructions* items. Add further items as you come across them, or as you find you are using them yourself, or as the students need them.

Variations

1 With a monolingual class whose language you know, ask students to say what they need to know how to say in English for classroom interaction; list their requests, and teach them systematically. The same applies to coursebook instructions: teach items like *Answer the questions* as you come across them. But in either case, note the need for reminders of the new items and review.
2 Have the classroom language you have taught in a permanent display on the classroom wall.

> ### ○ Teaching tip
>
> Having taught them, try to make sure that utterances, such as those listed here, are consistently said in English, and that students work out the meanings of coursebook instructions on their own. However, if you have a monolingual class whose language you know, more complex instructions are often best given in the L1.

Box 1.1.1: Classroom language

Useful interactive items for students to understand

- Listen/Read/Write/Talk about ...
- Do exercise ...
- Do you understand?
- Raise your hands.
- Sit down.
- Get into pairs/groups.
- Write in your notebooks ...
- Can I help you?

- Repeat ...
- Right/wrong
- Are you ready?
- Open your books at page ...
- Work with a friend.
- Work on your own.
- Is there a problem?
- Shall I say that again?

Useful interactive items for pupils to be able to say themselves

- I don't understand.
- What's the meaning of ...
- How do you say ... (L1) in English?
- What's another word for ... ?
- Excuse me!
- Please say it again.

- What page?
- I don't have (a pencil, a notebook, a book ...)
- Wait a minute, please!
- How do you spell ... ?
- I have a problem.

Coursebook, or classroom, instructions

- Complete the sentences.
- Complete the table.
- Underline the correct word/option.
- Circle the correct word/option.
- ... in brackets
- Turn ... into ...
- Write sentences.
- Match ...
- True or false?
- ... means the same as ... .

- Correct the sentences.
- Use the words ...
- Put the words in order.
- Read the text.
- Add ...
- Delete ...
- Answer the questions.
- ... in your notebook
- More than one answer is possible.

1.1.2 Word of the day

Outline	Students learn one new item at the beginning of a lesson.
Focus	Single words or expressions chosen by the teacher
Age	Pre-adolescent–Adult
Level	Any
Time	One minute

Procedure

1 Write on the board the heading *Word of the day* (or have it ready when the students enter the class).
2 Write and say the new word you want to teach: preferably one that is connected to one of the students in the class, or to yourself, or to something in the news.
3 Find out if anyone knows the meaning; if they don't, explain it.
4 Leave it up in a corner of the board, come back to remind students of it at the end of the lesson.

Variations

1 Use a *multi-word chunk*, or *proverb*, or *quotation*, instead of a single word. To find such items, check out websites like http://www.quotationspage.com/subjects/ or http://www.oneliners-and-proverbs.com/.
2 Combine with activities like *1.1.3 Show and tell!* so that the responsibility for thinking up a word of the day doesn't fall only on you!

Note

This makes a nice opening routine for lessons.

1.1.3 Show and tell!

Outline	Students teach other students words they know.
Focus	Single isolated words chosen by students
Age	Pre-adolescent–Adult
Level	Any
Time	Two or three minutes for each presentation

Procedure

1 Tell students that in each lesson one student will teach the rest of the class a new word or expression in English that he or she knows but (probably) nobody else does. They may get their new items from the Internet, from their families, from their reading, from a movie, or from wherever they like. This is their homework for today, though they may only present their word later in the course.

2 If there is already, in the present lesson, a student in the class who happens to know such an item, invite them to present it. If not, perhaps teach one yourself (see *1.1.2 Word of the day*).

3 In later lessons (it doesn't have to be every single lesson) invite individuals to teach 'their' new item. Usually, it's enough for one or two students to present in each lesson.

4 Encourage them to make their teaching more interesting by using pictures, examples, internet references and so on.

💡 **Teaching tip**

When allowing students to choose their own items to teach, you may in some cases need to make it clear in advance that they are not allowed to choose items that are 'taboo', or that might embarrass or distress members of the class (including you).

1.1.4 How do you say it in English?

Outline	Students learn vocabulary items they want to know.
Focus	Single isolated words or expressions chosen by students
Age	Adolescent–Adult
Level	Any
Time	Two or three minutes
Preparation	Tell students that they should note, in their own language, between lessons, any vocabulary they needed to use but didn't know, or which they think they would like to know.

Procedure

1 Invite a student to tell you in their own language what the word is that he or she wants to know. Provide the English translation if you can. If you don't know the student's language, note down the word and find out later, or enlist the help of another student.

2 Use the opportunity to teach another, linked, expression, or other ways to say the same sort of thing.

Variation

Do the reverse: invite students to bring words they heard or read in English but didn't understand, for you to explain in class. Note, however, that it's quite difficult to recall and present new items that were heard, as we tend simply not to *perceive* or be able to repeat vocabulary we didn't understand. Unknown words encountered during reading are easier to note down and present later.

Note

As with the previous two activities, this makes a nice routine element in your meetings with the class. Use it at the beginning, at the end, or as a 'filler' between longer components of the lesson.

1.1.5 Areas of expertise

Outline	Students make presentations about their areas of expertise to the rest of the class. This activity is particularly appropriate for courses in English for Specific Purposes (for example, Business English, Academic English).
Focus	Items from a specific area of knowledge
Age	Adult
Level	Intermediate–Advanced
Time	20 minutes
Preparation	Find out about professions or hobbies of individual students, and tell them to be ready to tell the class about them. They may ask you for any vocabulary they need in advance.

Procedure

1 Agree with one of the students in advance that they will present their area of expertise in a particular lesson.
2 Present the student and topic formally to the class, as if he or she were giving a presentation in a conference.
3 The student tells the members of the class about their area of expertise, teaching them new vocabulary that is needed. Either the student or you should write this vocabulary up on the board.
4 At the end of the presentation, invite other students to ask questions.
5 Thank the presenter, and get the class to applaud!
6 Review any useful vocabulary that was taught in the course of the presentation, using the items that have earlier been written on the board.

Follow-up

Make a note of any other words that the student might have found useful in their presentation and present them.

1.2 BUILDING ON CONTEXTS AND ASSOCIATIONS

These activities build on associations with situations, contexts, or vocabulary items that students already know. Paul Meara's book *Connected Words* (see *References and further reading*) contains some interesting articles on the association of words with one another as a way into vocabulary acquisition.

1.2.1 How many more can you think of?

Outline	Students add further items to lexical sets they already know.
Focus	Single words grouped in lexical sets
Age	Any
Level	Beginner–Intermediate
Time	Ten minutes
Preparation	A list of superordinates such as those in *Box 1.2.1*.

Procedure

1   Write on the board in large letters the name of a category that has a number of members (a superordinate): for example *Colours*. (see *Box 1.2.1* for some more suggestions.) Make sure all the class understand it.
2   Write up two or three words that might be members of this category (*hyponyms*) and that you are sure students know: for example *red, yellow, green*.

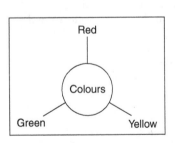 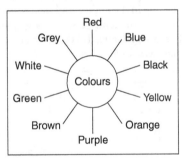

3   Invite the class to suggest in an open brainstorming session what other words might belong to this set. Write up those they contribute.
4   Add a few more yourself, and teach them.
5   Note down the complete list for yourself as a basis for the follow-up below, or for future review.

Follow-ups

1   Count how many items there are. Then delete them all (or just hide them, if you are using an interactive whiteboard), and see how many the class – and you! – can immediately recall, orally. Remind them of the ones they forgot.

2   Or – simpler – delete only some of the letters from each item, and challenge students to complete them.

Box 1.2.1: How many more can you think of?

- animals
- buildings
- clothes
- colours
- drink
- emotions, moods
- family

- food
- furniture
- machines
- moods
- parts of the body
- people
- professions

- shapes
- sizes
- sports
- things in the classroom
- the weather
- transport
- verbs of movement

 Teaching tip

The conventional way to make lists on the board is in vertical columns under a heading at the top. For brainstorms, however, it can be better to put the heading in the middle and then scatter the brainstormed items all around, joined to the centre by a 'sun-ray' pattern of lines, as shown in this activity. For more advanced classes, the sun-ray can be further expanded to a 'mind map' as shown below.

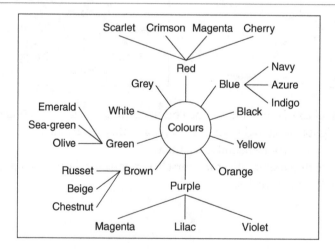

1.2.2 Brainstorm round a theme

Outline	A more sophisticated and complex version of the previous activity, suitable for more advanced students
Focus	Items associated with a particular topic or theme
Age	Pre-adolescent–Adult
Level	Intermediate–Advanced
Time	10–15 minutes
Preparation	A list of abstract themes, such as those in *Box 1.2.2*

Procedure

1 Write in the middle of the board in big letters a topic or theme you are interested in exploring. For example:

   MOVEMENT

   (For other ideas see *Box 1.2.2.*)

2 Suggest a few items that might relate to this concept that you think the class already know, and write them up around it: for example *slowly, a race, speed, into, through, get out, go away*. Make sure that you don't limit yourself to one part of speech, and include *chunks* (multi-word expressions) as well as single words.

3 Invite students to suggest some more items, and write them up.

4 Add any more useful ones that you'd like the class to know.

5 Check everyone understands all the items on the board.

Variation

Invite students to work first in pairs or small groups and come up with as many ideas as they can; then bring them together and elicit ideas in the full class.

Note

You can use this activity to familiarize students with the topic and vocabulary of the theme of a text you are going to work on, or as an introduction to a piece of literature.

Teaching tip

If you are getting a lot of ideas from the class in a brainstorm it can be very frustrating and time-wasting to go through the usual 'Be quiet, everyone, raise your hands . . . yes, Anna?' routine. Unless the class is a very unruly one, it's usually better just to let students call out ideas freely as they think of them, while you acknowledge and write them up as fast as you can: the process moves faster, more students participate, there are richer results, and the whole activity is more interesting to do.

Box 1.2.2: Brainstorm round a theme

- action
- authority
- autumn
- city
- cleanliness
- communication
- concert
- cooking
- exams
- fairy tales
- gardening
- home

- hospital
- language
- learning
- marriage
- movement
- night
- persuasion
- police
- quantity
- relationships
- road traffic
- shopping

- space
- speech
- spring
- storm
- summer
- technology
- time
- thought
- violence
- war
- winter
- work

1.2.3 Chain associations round the class

Outline	Students think of a word that associates with a previous word.
Focus	Words linked by free association
Age	Any
Level	Intermediate–Advanced
Time	10–15 minutes

Procedure

1 Say, and perhaps write up, one word that the class has recently learnt.
2 Invite a student to say what other concept this reminds them of, and say the word in English.
3 The next student says what this word reminds them of . . . and so on, round the class.
4 Tell the students that if another student says a word they don't know, they should raise their hand. When this happens, stop the association process for a moment, write the word on the board and explain or translate it.
5 If an association between the word a student says and the one before is not clear, ask the student to explain.
6 After a few minutes, stop and invite students to try to recall the chain of association backwards, from the last word to the first.
7 Check they remember the meanings of the words written on the board.

Variations

1 Students may contribute entire phrases or idioms rather than single words.
2 For more advanced classes: limit the associations to a particular theme.

Follow-up

Delete everything on the board, and challenge students to recall and write in their notebooks the entire chain of association. They can work in twos or threes. See if you can do the same yourself: get students to help you if you are stuck.

 Teaching tip

The principle of recalling items or sentences immediately after finishing an activity is a useful technique which can be used with almost any exercise. It provides a 'fun' challenge which also functions as a quick review.

1.2.4 Pass it round

Outline	Students add new items to lists of vocabulary as they are passed round the class.
Focus	Words that fit a given sentence context; collocations
Age	Any
Level	Beginner–Intermediate
Time	15 minutes
Preparation	Sheets of paper with 'base' items written halfway down. Use *Boxes 1.2.4a* and *b* or think of your own. You need one such sheet per three students, each showing a different item.

Procedure

1 Write on the board a base expression like:
    You can break ...

2 Invite students to suggest what objects might come after this, and add them like this:

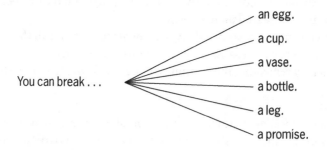

3 Divide the class into groups of three, give each a sheet of paper turned sideways, with a different beginning phrase:
    You can eat ...
    You can listen to ...
For some more suggestions as to what else you might use as 'cues' on these sheets, see *Box 1.2.4a*.

4 Tell students they have three minutes to fill in as many possible objects as they can. After three minutes, ring a bell, or call out *Stop!* and tell them to pass the sheet of paper to another group.

5 Each group now works on its new paper for three minutes: they have to read what the previous group has written and add more.

6 The process continues; make sure that each sheet of paper moves each time to a group which hasn't seen it before.

7   Move round the classroom helping groups think of new items; teach new words as necessary.

8   When all groups have contributed, students should leave the finished sheets on their desks and move round the class to read all the others.

9   Take in the sheets, and then either a), read out the results immediately, stopping to teach or review any items that some or all of the class don't know or b) take the lists home, and the next day go over any of the items you think the class may not have known, or needs to review.

Variations

1   With younger learners, tell each group to use a different-coloured pen or pencil. This way they can easily identify, when the activity is over, which group contributed what to each sheet (see *Follow-up* below).

2   Use negative instead of positive base expressions: *You can't eat . . .* etc.

3   Use combinations other than verb + object. For example, verb + adverb, or the reverse; adjective + noun or the reverse. See *Box 1.2.4b*.

4   Use the ideas that form the basis of *1.2.1 How many more can you think of?* or *1.2.2 Brainstorm round a theme.*

Follow-up

Particularly for younger classes: display the finished sheets on the wall.

Box 1.2.4a: Pass it round

Beginner

- You can agree with . . .
- You can allow . . .
- You can book . . .
- You can break . . .
- You can climb . . .
- You can cut . . .
- You can damage . . .
- You can discuss . . .
- You can drink . . .
- You can eat . . .
- You can educate . . .
- You can enjoy . . .

Intermediate/Advanced

- You can give back . . .
- You can hold . . .
- You can listen to . . .
- You can look after . . .
- You can oppose . . .
- You can organize . . .
- You can prepare . . .
- You can read . . .
- You can sit on . . .
- You can suffer from . . .
- You can understand . . .
- You can watch . . .

Box 1.2.4b: Pass it round

More possibilities

Adjectives (add nouns)
- hard . . . (for example, *question*)
- long . . . (for example, *way*)
- (a)bright . . . (for example, *colour*)

Nouns (add adjectives)
- a/an . . . book (for example, *interesting*)
- a/an . . . suggestion (for example, *useful*)
- a/an . . . animal (for example, *dangerous*)

Verbs (add adverbs)
- to drive . . . (for example, *carefully*)
- to shout . . . (for example, *angrily*)
- to speak . . . (for example, *softly*)

Adverbs (add verbs)
- to . . . clearly (for example, *explain*)
- to . . . slowly (for example, *walk*)
- to . . . rudely (for example, *answer*)

1.2.5 How else could you say it?

Outline	Students brainstorm different ways of expressing the same idea.
Focus	Synonyms, paraphrases
Age	Pre-adolescent–Adult
Level	Intermediate–Advanced
Time	15 minutes

Procedure

1 Select six or seven words or expressions that you have recently taught (from a text, or deriving from other activities in this section), and write them on the board.

2 Ask students if they know other words or expressions that mean more or less the same. Stress that these don't need to be very exact synonyms. For example, for *wife* you could accept *a married woman, a woman who has a husband*, but also *a member of the family*.

3 Write up any suggestions on the board, and add some more of your own; for example, for the above you might teach *spouse*.

Variation

Give step 2 above as homework. Students can ask friends or family, or look up the word in a thesaurus or dictionary of synonyms. Then you can do the 'pooling' process in the following lesson.

Notes

1 See 3.2.7 *Related words* for a more complex version of this activity leading to a wider range of associated items.

2 See 3.2.1 *It doesn't mean quite the same thing (1)* for a follow-up on this activity at a more advanced level, whose aim is to explore differences in meaning or connotation of apparent synonyms.

> **♀ Teaching tip**
>
> If your students have laptops or computers easily available in the classroom, they can use them to find synonyms or antonyms, using the thesaurus menu on Microsoft® Word or the equivalent.

1.2.6 Does it have an opposite?

Outline	Students learn new words as opposites of ones they already know.
Focus	Antonyms
Age	Adolescent–Adult
Level	Intermediate–Advanced
Time	15–20 minutes
Preparation	Slips of paper with 10–15 recently learnt words; dictionaries

Procedure

1 Give out slips of paper to students with a list of 10–15 words they have learnt this year; or simply dictate such a list for them to write down.
2 Challenge students to identify and mark with a tick (✓)which ones have opposites (even if they don't know how to say them in English).
3 They should then work individually or in pairs, writing as many opposites as they can to the 'ticked-off' items. If they don't know the opposite in English they should write it in their L1 or look it up in a dictionary (paper or digital) of synonyms and antonyms.
4 Discuss students' answers and add English translations where necessary.
5 Write up on the board all the opposites they have suggested.
6 Ask students to close their books or cover their notes, and challenge them to identify which original word matches each word you have written up.

Variation

With a more advanced class you may get into some interesting linguistic debate. For example, you may argue about whether a particular item has an opposite or not, and what it is. Does a verb like *run* have an opposite? If so, is it *walk? stop? stand still?* It doesn't matter if you don't come to a unanimously agreed conclusion: the main point is the discussion, exploration of meanings and the teaching of new items.

Note

Some words may have more than one opposite, because they contain within them more than one (implied) meaning. The opposite of *man*, for example, may be *boy* or *woman* (or *non-human* if you use *man* to mean *mankind*).

1.2.7 Which words do we know?

Outline	Students identify words they know in a new text.
Focus	Words learnt from a text
Age	Pre-adolescent–Adult
Level	Intermediate–Advanced
Time	15–20 minutes
Preparation	A text of less than one-page length that you are planning to study with the students

Procedure

1 Ask students to work in small groups of three or four. They read the text and underline everything they understand. More knowledgeable students teach the others any words they know that the others don't.

2 Having done that, the groups should talk about the main message of the text: what is it about?

3 Coming together in full class, make sure first that everyone understands the gist of the text.

4 Then ask each group to say one word or expression that was left not underlined: that they didn't understand, or were not sure of. If no other group can help them, explain it. Continue until all items have been explained.

Variation

Students underline words they don't know with a straight line, words they have seen before but don't understand with a squiggly line and words they can guess the meaning of with a dotted line. Then elicit and discuss each type of underlined item separately.

 Teaching tip

When beginning a new text, focus first on what the students do know, rather than what they don't. The conventional procedure which requires students to look first for unknown items in a new text belittles their present knowledge and makes it less likely that they'll be able to guess from context.

1.2.8 Vocabulary from a picture

Outline	Students learn new vocabulary through describing a picture.
Focus	Items that can be visually represented
Age	Young–Adolescent
Level	Beginner–Intermediate
Time	15–20 minutes
Preparation	One of the pictures shown in *Boxes 1.2.8 a, b, c* and *d* copied for students, or any picture with multiple components

Procedure

1 Invite students to study the picture and jot down all the words and expressions they think they would need in order to describe it. They don't need to write complete sentences: just single items. If there's anything they need but don't know how to say in English, they should write it in L1.
2 Students should now join together in threes and share their lists. They may help each other with translations where needed, and add any further items they think of.
3 Finally, invite students to pool their ideas. As they say them, write them up on the board and explain, or provide new items, as necessary. The board should end up full of both new and previously known vocabulary.

Variations

1 If students have dictionaries, they may use them at step 2 above.
2 After step 2, invite each group to combine with another to make a bigger group, and combine their lists, before the full-class pooling.
3 Each group counts how many items it has: who has the most?
4 Write up the pool of words and expressions on a big sheet of paper, and then display side-by-side with the picture on the classroom wall.
5 Instead of writing the words separately, invite students to stick them on the picture, using sticky Post-it™ labels.

Follow-up

Students write descriptions of the picture, using as much of the vocabulary they have pooled as they can.

> **Teaching tip**
>
> Where an activity results in a joint written product of some kind written on paper, it is useful to post this on the wall of the classroom, so that students continue to be exposed to the lexical items. You can also use such displays later as the basis for review.

Box 1.2.8a: Vocabulary from a picture

From *Vocabulary Activities* © Cambridge University Press 2012   PHOTOCOPIABLE

Box 1.2.8b: Vocabulary from a picture

From *Vocabulary Activities* © Cambridge University Press 2012   PHOTOCOPIABLE

Box 1.2.8c: Vocabulary from a picture

From *Vocabulary Activities* © Cambridge University Press 2012   PHOTOCOPIABLE

Box 1.2.8d: Vocabulary from a picture

From *Vocabulary Activities* © Cambridge University Press 2012   PHOTOCOPIABLE

1.2.9 Abbreviated txt

Outline	Students learn and use abbreviated text forms for email, chat, tweeting and SMS texting.
Focus	Abbreviated forms such as 'gr8'
Age	Any
Level	Beginner–Intermediate
Time	15–20 minutes
Preparation	Abbreviated text as in *Box 1.2.9a* copied for students or displayed on the board

Procedure

1 Display or distribute the text shown in *Box 1.2.9a*.
2 Give students a couple of minutes to read and discuss it with partners.
3 In full class, translate the text into normal written English. You may need to help the class with this, using *Answers (Box 1.2.9a)* as some of the items are not 'transparent'.
4 Discuss. Which abbreviations did the students know? Which didn't they? Note that they probably won't have known CWOT: an example of why NOT to use abbreviations unless you're sure your reader knows them.
5 Brainstorm on the board other abbreviations the class knows; add any more you know yourself, or from *Box 1.2.9b*.
6 Hold a brief discussion on the use of such abbreviations, making sure students are aware of the following points:
   • These abbreviations are suitable only for very informal texts (emails, text messages, chats, tweets, some blogs); they should not be used in other kinds of writing.
   • They are used relatively little, in fact; and quite a lot of people are not aware of what they mean, so it's safer to use the full forms unless you are sure your reader is familiar with them!
   • Some abbreviations tend to 'date': they are current for a while and then fall into disuse.
   • They are mainly used by teenagers and young adults.

Note

If you want to learn more abbreviations used in text, chat and emails, have a look at the LG site http://www.lgdtxtr.com/, and/or send your students to check it out.

Box 1.2.9a: Abbreviated txt

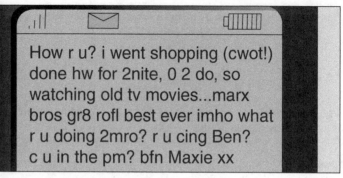

How r u? i went shopping (cwot!)
done hw for 2nite, 0 2 do, so
watching old tv movies...marx
bros gr8 rofl best ever imho what
r u doing 2mro? r u cing Ben?
c u in the pm? bfn Maxie xx

Answers (Box 1.2.9a Abbreviated txt)

How are you? I went shopping (complete waste of time!), done homework for tonight, nothing to do, so watching old TV movies . . . Marx Brothers, great, rolling on the floor laughing, best ever in my humble opinion. What are you doing tomorrow? Are you seeing Ben? See you in the afternoon? Bye for now, Maxie.

Box 1.2.9b: Abbreviated txt

Types of text abbreviation

1 **Lack of capitalization:**
   i (for the pronoun *I*)   english

2 **Missing letters (especially vowels):**
   txt (=text)   msg (=message)   nt (=not)   cn (=can)   aftr (= after)

3 **Simplified spelling:**
   fone (=phone)   nite (=night)   rite (=right/write)

4 **Use of symbols:**
   & (=and)   @ (=at)

5 **Single letters or numbers to represent words or morphemes:**
   b (=be)   c (=see)   r (=are)   u (=you)   2 (=to/too)
   4 (=for/fore-)   8 (=-ate)

6 **Common abbreviations**
   asap (=as soon as possible)   bfn (=bye for now)   btw (=by the way)
   f2f (=face to face)   fyi (=for your information,   gr8 (=great)
   imho (=in my humble/honest opinion)   lol (=laughing out loud)

1.2.10 Places and things you do there

Outline	Students describe what is done in different places and present their ideas to the class.
Focus	Verb phrases describing activities
Age	Adolescent–Adult
Level	Beginner–Intermediate
Time	30 minutes
Preparation	Pictures of locations as shown in *Box 1.2.10*; or just their names, copied for students

Procedure

1 Write up the name of the institution where your present course is taking place and ask students to tell you what people do there. They will start with obvious things like: *teach, study, give lectures, read books, get grades*; but encourage them to think beyond such ideas to 'extra-curricular' activities such as *drink coffee, have snacks, gossip*. Teach new vocabulary as needed.

2 Divide the class into four groups and give one picture from *Box 1.2.10* (or just the name of a place) to each.

3 The group elects two secretaries. Members of the group then 'brainstorm' as many things as they can that people do in the place they have been allotted. The secretaries write down the ideas, sharing the writing load between them, but may also contribute ideas of their own.

4 You meanwhile go round the different groups, suggesting other things they might add, and teaching new vocabulary in the process.

5 Each group presents its place and activities to the class, teaching the other students any new vocabulary they have learnt.

Variations

1 This activity can also be done using the technique described in *1.2.4 Pass it round*.

2 A similar brainstorm can be built around events, described in words rather than pictures: a wedding, a birthday party, a political demonstration. Or things: What can you do with . . . a pen, a tablecloth, a teaspoon, a piece of paper, a cup?

Box 1.2.10: Places and things you do there

Shopping mall

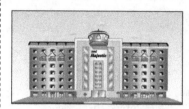

Hotel

Farm

Home

School

Hospital

Beach

Theatre

1.2.11 What other meanings does it have?

Outline	Students look for further meanings of words they have previously learnt.
Focus	Polysemous words (words that have multiple meanings); words with extended metaphorical meanings
Age	Adolescent–Adult
Level	Intermediate–Advanced
Time	15 minutes
Preparation	Dictionaries

Procedure

1   Choose a word that the class has come across or used recently. This doesn't necessarily have to be a recently taught one, but should be one which you know has further meanings besides that which the class already knows. It could be something as simple as *table* (the piece of furniture, or a type of data display) or *blue* (the colour, or unhappy) or *run* (move quickly, or manage).

2   Remind the class of the basic meaning of the word. Ask if anyone knows any further meanings.

3   Tell them to look the word up in the dictionary and find at least one other meaning, besides what has already been learnt.

4   Students work for another five minutes, looking for additional meanings for at least one other word they have in their vocabulary notebooks.

5   Students share their findings in full class.

Follow-ups

1   Students look up the word in a corpus (using the *British National Corpus* at http://corpus.byu.edu/bnc/, or the *American Corpus of Contemporary English* at http://www.americancorpus.org/, or the *Lextutor* corpus concordance at http://www.lextutor.ca/concordancers/concord_e.html) and find contexts for the word used in its different meanings (phrases or full sentences). They then present these to the rest of the class, and also tell them which, in their search, they found to be most frequent.

2   A simpler alternative is to use the websites *ForBetterEnglish* http://forbetterenglish.com/ (which supplies a full-sentence example for each use) or *Just the Word* http://www.just-the-word.com/, which supplies phrases and collocations and the frequency of their occurrence in the *British National Corpus*.

Variations

1 Base the activity on three or four words instead of one.
2 If they don't have dictionaries easily available, tell students the new meanings yourself (but check the dictionary first to make sure you've remembered all the useful ones!).
3 Ask students to look not only for meanings but also for whole phrases that use the word.

Note

The *Cambridge Advanced Learner's Dictionary* (http://dictionary.cambridge.org/) and some other good learner dictionaries give different meanings of words as separate entries, which makes this searching process much easier.

 Teaching tip

It's important for each student to have their own dictionary – or, if they have individual laptops, tablets or mobile phones with internet access, a dictionary web address easily accessible on the 'favorites/bookmarks' menu.

1.2.12 Same word, different part of speech (1)

Outline	Students write sentences to show how words are used in different parts of speech.
Focus	Similar words used as different parts of speech
Age	Adolescent–Adult
Level	Intermediate–Advanced
Time	30 minutes
Preparation	One of the sets of lists shown in *Boxes 1.2.12a* and *b*, selected according to the level of your class and copied for students or displayed on the board; dictionaries

Procedure

1   Tell students that one of the ways English expands its vocabulary is to take a simple lexical item – a noun, verb, adjective or adverb – and use it, as it stands, as a different part of speech. Give some simple examples: *to run* (v), *a run* (n); *orange* (adj), *an orange* (n); *fast* (adj), *fast* (adv). Tell them that this exercise focuses on the noun/verb or verb/noun conversion.

2   Give out the lists you have prepared, and talk the students through two or three of them, showing how the conversion works, and providing or eliciting sample sentences to highlight the differences. For example, for the item *nail* the contrasting sentences might be:

> The carpenter used nails (noun).
> He nailed the picture to the wall (verb).

3   Tell students to work in pairs and compose similar pairs of sentences for at least six of the items in another list. They may use dictionaries if available.

4   Any pair who finishes a list should try to think of more items that would fit the same category and could also be used in different parts of speech. Again, they may use dictionaries – or consult you!

Variations

1   Instead of students thinking up more items as they finish, you may ask them to go on to work on another list on their sheet.

2   Focus on the specific aspect of pronunciation. Some Latinate words are spelt the same whether they are nouns or verbs but are pronounced

differently, with the stress on the first syllable if they are nouns, and on the second if they are verbs. You may find the list shown in *Box 1.2.12c* useful . Occasionally the actual sounds may change: words like *use* and *house* have an unvoiced /s/ when they are nouns, but a voiced /z/ when they are verbs.

Notes

1 The most common conversion is noun to adjective: most nouns can be used as noun modifiers which are virtual adjectives (a *computer* program, a *vegetable* knife, etc.). This counts as a grammatical rule of the language, and does not need focused practice in vocabulary expansion activities like this one. The conversions listed here are item-specific (not all lexical words can convert in this way), and therefore need to be learnt.

2 For our purposes it does not really matter whether a noun or verb came first, historically, in a particular case. If a student perceives a word as a noun, when etymologically speaking it was first a verb, this need not worry us: the main thing is that they should be aware of its different potential functions.

♀ Teaching tip

Teach students to identify the signs for words stress in their dictionaries: usually there is a ' sign before the stressed syllable, but sometimes learners' dictionaries use upper-case letters or underlining.

Box 1.2.12a: Same word, different part of speech (1)

For intermediate classes

Objects with a function

- alarm
- brake
- brush
- clip
- hammer
- knife
- nail
- pin
- rope
- spoon
- tape
- wheel

Containers

- bag
- bottle
- box
- cage
- can
- envelope
- package
- pocket
- shelf

Parts of the body

- arm
- elbow
- eye
- foot
- hand
- head
- knee
- shoulder
- skin
- stomach

Applying a substance

- butter
- flour
- grease
- ice
- oil
- paint
- paper
- soap
- spread
- sugar
- water

Continued

Box 1.2.12a (*continued*)

People and their functions

- boss
- captain
- cook
- doctor
- guard
- judge
- master
- nurse
- pilot
- police

Actions and feelings

- bow
- break
- dance
- feel
- hate
- jump
- kiss
- love
- push
- shock
- swim
- wash

Technological functions

- blog
- chat
- email
- Google™
- (hyper)link
- Photoshop®
- podcast
- text
- Twitter/tweet

Box 1.2.12b: Same word, different part of speech (1)

For advanced classes

Objects with a function	
• axe	• motor
• brake	• needle
• chisel	• saddle
• harness	• shovel
• mask	• thread
• mirror	

People and their functions	
• apprentice	• mother
• author	• pioneer
• broker	• queen
• coach	• referee
• father	• slave

- -

Containers	
• bin	• file
• cradle	• net
• crate	• pigeonhole
• dish	• sheath
• drain	• slot

Actions and feelings	
• ache	• embrace
• caress	• envy
• caution	• leap
• comfort	• prize
• desire	• reward
• detour	• shiver

From *Vocabulary Activities* © Cambridge University Press 2012   PHOTOCOPIABLE

Box 1.2.12c: Same word, different part of speech (1)

Some words which change their stress

• absent	• export	• produce
• abstract	• import	• progress
• conduct	• increase	• reject
• contrast	• object	• subject
• convert	• present	• transport
• decrease		

From *Vocabulary Activities* © Cambridge University Press 2012   PHOTOCOPIABLE

1.2.13 Same word, different part of speech (2)

Outline	Students use the dictionary to find further meanings for words in different parts of speech.
Focus	Words which can be used as different parts of speech
Age	Adolescent–Adult
Level	Intermediate–Advanced
Time	20 minutes
Preparation	Dictionaries

Procedure

1 Invite students to look at the latest text the class has studied, pick out ten nouns, verbs and adjectives whose meaning they understand, and write them down.

2 Give the students ten minutes to look up their words in the dictionary to find out which of them can be used as a different part of speech, and if so what exactly they mean.

3 After ten minutes, elicit results. Were there any surprises? Were there any items which had more than one corresponding word in another part of speech?

1.2.14 Words that are the same in my language

Outline	Students compete to find who can find the most cognates: words in their language that are the same as, or similar to, words in English. This activity is appropriate for classes whose members share the same mother tongue, but can also be done by multilingual classes (see *Variation*).
Focus	Cognates (words in the students' mother tongue that are similar to ones in English)
Age	Pre-adolescent–Adult
Level	Any
Time	15 minutes
Preparation	For yourself: a list of all the cognates you can think of common to English and the students' L1 (See *Box 1.2.14* for a list of words that are used both in English and in a variety of other languages; use it as a basis for your own list, deleting and adding words as appropriate.)

Procedure

1 Put students into small groups, with one 'secretary' whose job it is to write down the words.
2 Tell them they have five minutes to compile a list of as many words as they can that are used in their mother tongue, and which they know come from, or are also used in, English. Tell students that it's a competition: which group can find the most?
3 At the end of the five minutes, ask each group how many words it has: the group with the most words is Winner No. 1. (there will be another!)
4 One group's secretary reads out their list. Any item which another group has also written can be ticked off, by all the groups who have it. So the first group is left with a set of 'unticked' words which no other group has.
5 Repeat the process with other groups.
6 As you do steps 4 and 5 above, explain (and note down for later review) any words which not all the class know.
7 The group with the most 'unticked' words is Winner no. 2.

Variations

1 If your class is multilingual, invite students to work in small groups with classmates who have different mother tongues, and tell each other about words in their own languages that they know are similar to English

ones, or borrowed from English. Later, groups tell the rest of the class about some of the words they found.

2 For more advanced students, limit them to a particular area to look for cognates. You might suggest one of the following: music; food and cooking; academic subjects of study; clothes; technology; animals and plants; science; medicine; sport.

Follow-ups

1 For homework, ask students to find more cognates by asking friends or family, or by looking on the Internet, and bring findings to the next lesson.

2 With younger classes, invite each group to make colourful posters to put up on the class wall showing all the cognates they have found. It doesn't matter if some items are repeated in different posters.

Notes

1 The 'ticking off' process enables you to go through all the words, teaching or reviewing any that were not familiar to some members of the class.

2 Probably most of the words students find will be loan words that their language has absorbed from English; but a few may be the reverse: words that English has taken from the students' language. It may be interesting – and morale-boosting – to identify these! Yet others may have come both to English and to the students' mother tongue from a third language.

3 If you are interested in finding out, and perhaps telling your students, what language a particular word originally came from and how it entered English, look it up in the *Online Etymological Dictionary* http://www.etymonline.com/.

Box 1.2.14: Words that are the same in my language

- album
- alcohol
- algebra
- alibi
- ambulance
- ammonia
- antenna
- antibody
- atlas
- auditorium
- automatic
- avocado
- balloon
- banana
- bank
- bass
- caravan
- chaos
- charisma
- chef
- chocolate
- coffee
- comedy
- concert
- crocodile
- crystal
- dragon
- dialogue
- diploma
- disk

- dolphin
- allergy
- aluminum
- festival
- golf
- helicopter
- hello
- ideal
- incubator
- index
- instinct
- insulin
- intensive
- intercom
- inertia
- irony
- jeans
- ketchup
- malaria
- mango
- marathon
- mathematics
- museum
- opera
- optimist
- ping-pong
- plastic
- pop
- problem
- professor

- pyjamas
- radar
- republic
- sandal
- seminar
- shampoo
- ski
- soda
- solo
- soprano
- sport
- standard
- stereo
- student
- symphony
- tango
- tank
- taxi
- tea
- telephone
- television
- terrorist
- toast
- toffee
- tractor
- ultimatum
- video
- vitamin

1.2.15 It's the same in my language – or is it?

Outline	Students check they know the differences between words that are apparently the same in English but in fact mean something else. This activity is appropriate for classes whose members share the same mother tongue, but can also be done by multilingual classes.
Focus	False friends
Age	Adolescent–Adult
Level	Intermediate–Advanced
Time	10–15 minutes
Preparation	A list of 'false friends' (between English and the students' mother tongue). Some common false friends with various other languages are listed in *Box 1.2.15* but you will, of course, need to adapt this list for your class, adding and deleting items as appropriate before copying it for students.

Procedure

1   Give out the lists of false friends and ask students to fill in as many meanings as they can. They may write the meanings in L1 or in English, according to the level of the class. They may work individually or in pairs.
2   Check and correct in full-class discussion.

Variation

In multilingual classes, invite students in small mixed groups to compare the false friends they found between their own language(s) and English.

Box 1.2.15: It's the same in my language – or is it?

	Meaning of a similar word in my language	Meaning in English
actual		
ancient		
assist		
attend		
become		
bizarre		
demand		
etiquette		
handy		
normal		
pretend		
realize		
sensible		
sympathetic		

From *Vocabulary Activities* © Cambridge University Press 2012   PHOTOCOPIABLE

1.2.16 Woof! Woof!

Outline	Students identify animals through saying their noises in English.
Focus	Names of animals and their noises
Age	Young
Level	Beginner
Time	20 minutes (distributed over two lessons)
Preparation	Pictures of animals, copied for students. Use *Box 1.2.16a* or your own images.

Procedure

1   Distribute the pictures of animals, and teach or review their names in English.

2   Ask students to tell you what each animal says, in their L1. Teach them the English equivalent as shown in *Box 1.2.16b* (which often sounds funny to them!). They don't write them down, but simply try to remember them orally.

3   Review the noises in the following lesson, and then play the following game:

  • Tell them you are an English speaker who only knows the sounds of the animals in English.

  • A student volunteers an animal sound: if you 'understand' it and can guess the animal, the class gets a tick (✓), which you write on the board. If you can't, they get a cross (✗), which cancels a tick. The aim is for the class to get up to ten ticks.

  • If there are any sounds you've found that nobody manages to get right, remind them of these at the end of the game.

Follow-up

For older students, you might also teach the various verbs which describe animal noises; see *Box 1.2.16b*.

Box 1.2.16a: Woof! Woof!

From *Vocabulary Activities* © Cambridge University Press 2012   PHOTOCOPIABLE

Box 1.2.16b: Woof! Woof!

Animal	Sound	Verb
bee	buzz	buzz
bird	cheep, tweet	chirrup, sing
cat	miaow, purr	mew, purr
cock/rooster	cock a doodle doo	crow
cow	moo	low
crow	caw caw	croak
dog	woof woof, grr	bark, growl
donkey	hee-haw	bray
duck	quack	quack
owl	to-whit, to-whoo	hoot
pig	oink	grunt
sheep	baa	bleat

1.3 FOCUS ON WORD COMBINATIONS

These activities provide tasks for learning vocabulary items that consist of multi-word chunks.

1.3.1 What usually goes with this word? (1)

Outline	Students use dictionaries to find common collocations of a given word.
Focus	Collocations
Age	Adolescent–Adult
Level	Intermediate–Advanced
Time	20 minutes
Preparation	Monolingual English dictionaries whose entries include samples of the headword in context

Procedure

1 Teach the students the meaning of the word *collocation*: the tendency a word has to co-occur with another word. For example, *take/make* collocate with *a decision* (you can't *have, do* or *get* a decision). Explain the following points:

   • Collocations may involve all sorts of parts of speech, not just nouns, adjectives, verbs and adverbs. They include the most common prepositions that come after, or precede, a target word: for example, *afraid of* or *at six o'clock*.

   • The components of a collocation may not occur next to each other: we can say **take** *a very difficult* **decision** or *at about six o'clock*.

2 Show students how collocations are indicated in a sample dictionary entry: for example, the entry for *foreign* in the *Cambridge Advanced Learners's Dictionary* (*Box 1.3.1*). Explain that they will just need to pick up some collocations from the sample sentences in dictionaries (for example, *foreign language*); others are explicitly shown in bold font (**foreign to, foreign affairs**).

3 Select single words that have recently been taught in class.

4 Give students ten minutes to look up the words in their dictionaries and try to identify at least one collocation for each.

5 After ten minutes, ask students to say what they have found, and write the resulting collocations up on the board.

6 Elicit a few sentences that are true or relevant for the students themselves or the present situation (in or beyond the classroom!), that contextualize the collocations.

Variations

1 Give step 4 above (looking up in the dictionaries) as homework, and then share the resulting findings in the following lesson.

2 Do step 6 as a separate individual, pair or group activity.

♀ Teaching tip

In activities that focus on dictionary use, it's preferable to use published (paper or CD-ROM) dictionaries, rather than websites that invite you to 'look up a word' in their dictionary. Such websites may show only a shortened version of the entry provided in the published version.

Box 1.3.1: What usually goes with this word? (1)

foreign /'fɒr.ən/ ⓤ /'fɔːr-/ *adjective* **1** Ⓔ belonging or connected to a country which is not your own: *Spain was the first foreign country she had visited.* ○ *foreign languages* ○ *His work provided him with the opportunity for a lot of foreign travel.* **2 foreign to** FORMAL Something can be described as foreign to a particular person if they do not know about it or it is not within their experience: *The whole concept of democracy, she claimed, was utterly foreign to the present government.* **3** describes an object or substance which has entered something else, possibly by accident, and does not belong there: *a foreign object/substance* ○ *foreign matter*

,**foreign af'fairs** *plural noun* matters that are connected with other countries

,**foreign 'aid** *noun* [U] the help that is given by a richer country to a poorer one, usually in the form of money or food

1.3.2 What usually goes with this word? (2)

Outline	Students search a corpus to find common collocations of a given word.
Focus	Collocations
Age	Adolescent–Adult
Level	Advanced
Time	40–50 minutes
Preparation	Computers with access to the Internet

Procedure

1 Teach the students the meaning of the word *collocation* (see the previous activity, step 1).

2 Allot each student a different word that has been recently taught.

3 Tell each student to find out which other words or expressions most often collocate with their words, using a corpus. Use the *British National Corpus* (http://corpus.byu.edu/bnc/) or the *American Corpus of Contemporary English* (http://www.americancorpus.org/). Type in the target word in the *words* box, and then click on *collocates* beneath it. Clicking on *search* will provide all the collocations found in the corpus, in order of frequency of occurrence. Clicking on the number (under the *TOT* heading) will give actual examples in context.

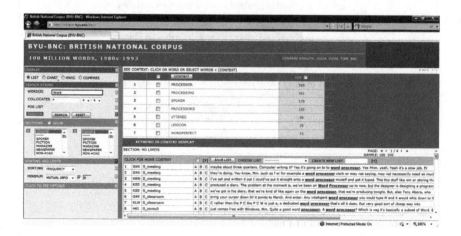

4　Students then choose the collocations they feel are most useful and important ones to learn (usually, but not always, the most common), and make a printed list or poster, with examples in context.

5　Post the lists on the classroom wall, and invite students to 'browse' and note down any new or interesting collocations.

Variations

1　Instead of using a corpus, invite students to Google™ the target item and look at the kinds of phrases shown on the resulting pages. They can also Google™ whole collocations framed in double quotation marks to find how much, and how, the target collocation is used in web texts. This, however, will only provide the exact formulation you've written: so, for example, "take a decision" will not provide instances of *took a decision* or *take a good decision*.

2　A simpler alternative is to use a website that directly provides lists of collocations of a keyword based on a corpus: for example, *ForBetterEnglish* http://forbetterenglish.com/ or *Just the Word* http://www.just-the-word.com/. *ForBetterEnglish* also provides a sentence example for each collocation, but neither website gives the more comprehensive sets of contexts provided by the corpus sites referred to earlier. Just clicking on the word without requesting *collocates* at either of the corpus websites suggested above will provide a concordance of a number of occurrences of the word in context. Students can then get an impression of the typical contexts in which a word occurs.

Note

This activity results in richer and more 'authentic' results than the dictionary-based procedure described in the previous activity, but is more time consuming.

 Teaching tip

With open-ended tasks that could be very much more, or less, time-consuming for different students, it's a good idea to give a time limit: 'See what you can do in twenty minutes' rather than 'Do ten (or any other fixed number) items.' This saves you having to hang around waiting for the slower workers, or finding things to occupy the faster ones. It is also a useful instruction to apply to homework assignments.

1.3.3 Identifying lexical phrases

Outline	Students identify words in a text that go together to make phrases or compound words.
Focus	Lexical phrases, compound words
Age	Adolescent–Adult
Level	Intermediate–Advanced
Time	20–30 minutes
Preparation	Text A shown in *Box 1.3.3*, displayed or copied for students

Procedure

1 Explain to students that we often learn vocabulary as multi-word phrases or even sentences that have a global meaning and that we learn by heart as a single *chunk*. Give some examples:

> to call it a day
> by the way
> How are you?
> It doesn't matter.

2 Discuss with students which items might be considered *chunks* in the text shown in *Box 1.3.3*. Students then do the same with a text from their course materials. They may work in pairs or small groups. Go round helping them, if they are uncertain which combinations count as *chunks*. Note that what exactly qualifies as a *chunk* is fairly vague: your own intuitions are probably the best guide here.

 Teaching tip

When students are noting down new words in their vocabulary notebooks, encourage them to write these together with their most common collocations, including prepositions, rather than just the word on its own, for example, *afraid of* rather than just *afraid*.

Box 1.3.3: Identifying lexical phrases

Sherlock Holmes and Dr Watson go camping. They pitch their tent under the stars and go to sleep. Sometime in the middle of the night, Holmes wakes Watson up.

'Watson, look up at the stars and tell me what you deduce.'

Watson says: 'I see millions of stars. If there are millions of stars, and if even a few of them have planets, it's quite likely there are some planets like Earth; and if there are a few planets like Earth out there, there might also be life.'

Holmes replies: 'Watson, you idiot, someone stole our tent!'

From *Vocabulary Activities* © Cambridge University Press 2012   PHOTOCOPIABLE

Answers (Box 1.3.3 Identifying lexical phrases)

Sherlock Holmes and Dr Watson *go camping*. They *pitch (their) tent* under the stars and *go to sleep*. Sometime *in the middle of the night*, Holmes *wakes (Watson) up*.

'Watson, *look up* at the stars and *tell me* what you deduce.'

Watson says: 'I see *millions of* stars. If *there are millions of* stars, and if even *a few of (them)* have planets, *it's (quite) likely* there are some planets like Earth; and if there are *a few planets* like Earth *out there*, there might also be life.'

Holmes replies: 'Watson, you idiot, someone stole our tent!'

1.3.4 Paired expressions

Outline	Students recall missing items from paired expressions.
Focus	Paired expressions with *and* or *or*
Age	Pre-adolescent–Adult
Level	Beginner–Intermediate
Time	Ten minutes
Preparation	A selection of expressions from *Box 1.3.4*, displayed for students

Procedure

1 Write up on the board ten or fifteen paired expressions from *Box 1.3.4*. Make sure they all have the same linking word in the middle (*and* or *or*).
2 Invite students to ask you if there are any expressions whose meaning is not clear, and explain as needed.
3 Tell students to close their eyes. Delete the first or second item from each paired expression.
4 Tell students to open their eyes and see if they can reconstruct the missing items. They may talk to each other and help each other remember, but don't need to write anything down.
5 Invite students to come to the board and write in the missing items.

Variations

1 At step 1, invite students to suggest any other paired expressions they happen to know, and add them.
2 For intermediate classes, the initial list may include both *or* and *and* expressions.
3 To make the activity more difficult, delete the *and* or *or* as well as one of the lexical items in the pair, and make sure that all words are written in lower case and scattered over the board (not in an aligned vertical list). The students then have to work out if the remaining word is the first or second of the pair and what the linking word is. (There may of course be cases where a word could be either the first or the second: for example, *here and there, there and then.*)
4 Another possibility is to delete the *and/or* and scatter the other words round the board. Students then try to pair them up.
5 Use the same technique (deleting one bit of an expression and eliciting the rest from the students) with any set of fixed expressions.
6 Use the paired expressions as the basis for a game of Pelmanism (see *2.1.10 Remembering pairs*).

Note

There are a few sentence endings to express *hedges* or vagueness in spoken English which are prefixed with *or* or *and* and which are worth learning as vocabulary items in themselves: *or something (someone, somewhere), or whatever, or not, or so, and so on, and the like.* You might take this opportunity to teach them.

 Teaching tip

If you are eliciting multiple answers and want to invite students to write these on the board themselves, it's a good idea to have two or three students writing at the same time. If it's only one at a time the process can become very slow and tedious and fewer students are likely to participate.

Box 1.3.4: Paired expressions

Selected expressions with *and*: Beginner

- before and after
- black and white
- come and go
- dos and don'ts
- each and every
- in and out

- ladies and gentlemen
- large and small
- mother and father
- one and only
- round and round
- there and then

- this and that
- top and bottom
- up and down
- where and when
- with and without
- yes and no

Selected expressions with *and*: Intermediate

- by and large
- bright and early
- far and away
- far and wide
- for and against
- forgive and forget

- hit and run
- live and let live
- off and on
- once and for all
- over and above

- pros and cons
- pure and simple
- safe and sound
- so and so
- whys and wherefores

Selected expressions with *or*: Beginner

- all or nothing
- in or out
- like it or not
- me or you
- more or less

- once or twice
- one or another
- one or more
- one or two
- some or all

- something or other
- this or that
- up or down
- yes or no

Selected expressions with *or*: Intermediate

- by hook or by crook
- fact or fiction
- for richer or poorer
- give or take

- right(ly) or wrong(ly)
- sink or swim
- sooner or later

- take it or leave it
- true or false
- whether or not

1.3.5 Comparing proverbs

Outline	Students compare English proverbs with ones in their mother tongue. This activity is appropriate for classes whose members share the same mother tongue, but can also be done by multilingual classes (see *Variation 2*).
Focus	Proverbs
Age	Adolescent–Adult
Level	Intermediate–Advanced
Time	20 minutes
Preparation	A selected list of proverbs, displayed on the board or copied for students; use some of those shown in *Box 1.3.5*, or a website such as *The Phrase Finder* (http://www.phrases.org.uk/meanings/proverbs.html) or *The Oxford Dictionary of Proverbs* (http://www.oxfordreference.com/)

Procedure

1 Give students a list of about ten to fifteen proverbs. You might select these deliberately so that most of them match proverbs from the students' L1, or simply give a random set.

2 Go through them in full class making sure that both their literal and figurative meanings are clear.

3 Ask students to work in pairs looking for mother-tongue proverbs that convey a similar message to the English one. If they can't find one, then they should simply translate into mother tongue.

4 Where students have found L1 parallels, discuss the similarities/differences in the metaphors used and in the basic message. Are there any proverbs in the students' L1 which actually contradict the English one?

Variations

1 Discuss the 'messages' of the proverbs: do the students agree with them? When might they be untrue? Do they convey a moral message, practical advice or simply a (sometimes cynical) truth?

2 Instead of steps 3 and 4 above, multilingual classes can work in mixed groups, telling each other about parallel proverbs in their own languages and comparing them with the English ones.

Vocabulary Activities

Follow-ups

1   Tell students to turn over their pages, and erase anything you
    have written on the board. How many of the proverbs you've just
    been working on can they remember and write out? When they've
    remembered all they can, they should check with the original list.
2   Invite students to change the beginnings or endings of any proverbs
    they like in order to make them more emphatic, more poetic, funnier or
    truer (for them!). For example, they might change *After rain comes fair
    weather to After rain comes mud.*
3   Ask the students if they know of any proverbs from their own language
    which have been translated into English.

Box 1.3.5: Comparing proverbs

- Absence makes the heart grow fonder.
- Actions speak louder than words.
- After rain comes fair weather.
- All cats are grey in the dark (in the night).
- All men can't be masters.
- All roads lead to Rome.
- Appearances are deceptive.
- Beauty is but skin-deep.
- Beggars can't be choosers.
- Blood is thicker than water.
- Business before pleasure.
- Curiosity killed the cat.
- Death pays all debts.
- Experience is the best teacher.
- Fine feathers make fine birds.
- Fools rush in where angels fear to tread.
- Honesty is the best policy.
- It's no use crying over spilt milk.
- Let sleeping dogs lie.
- Love is blind.
- Make hay while the sun shines.
- Man does not live by bread alone.
- Many hands make light work.
- Money is the root of all evil.
- Necessity is the mother of invention.
- New brooms sweep clean.
- No news is good news.
- Nothing succeeds like success.
- Pride goes before a fall.
- Silence is golden.
- Still waters run deep.
- Time and tide wait for no man.
- Time cures all things.
- Time is money.
- Time is the great healer.
- Truth is stranger than fiction.
- Walls have ears.
- While there's life there's hope.
- You can't teach old dogs new tricks.

1.3.6 Idioms and their meanings

Outline	Students guess the meaning of idiomatic items and check their answers.
Focus	Idioms
Age	Adolescent–Adult
Level	Intermediate–Advanced
Time	20 minutes
Preparation	A list of idioms, copied for students; use a selection from *Box 1.3.6*, or from a website such as http://www.idiomconnection.com/ or http://www.idiomsite.com/

Procedure

1 Explain to students what an *idiom* is: a figurative expression whose meaning cannot usually be guessed simply by knowing the meanings of its individual words. If you are working with a monolingual class, you might elicit or suggest idioms used in the students' L1.

2 Distribute a list of ten or fifteen English idioms you want to work on, and invite students to discuss for a few minutes, in small groups, what they think each means and in what context they might be used. Some they may already know; others may be relatively obvious. But there are likely to be a few which are unclear.

3 In full-class discussion, elicit some of the students' definitions and contexts. Approve, correct and teach new meanings as appropriate.

Follow-up

Ask students to write short stories that provide a context for one or more of the idioms learnt.

Notes

1 Similar idioms may exist in the students' mother tongue. Encourage students to compare and contrast the English idioms with L1 parallels.

2 If you add more idioms collected from a website or dictionary of idioms, make sure that these are ones that you yourself might actually use; a lot of idioms (*raining cats and dogs*, for example) are so rare that they aren't really worth teaching time, except for the most advanced classes. Others may be limited to a particular speech community and not used in international communicative English; again, probably not worth teaching.

Box 1.3.6: Idioms and their meanings

- Achilles' heel
- alive and kicking
- apple of somebody's eye
- be dead to the world
- be in hot water
- be in somebody's shoes
- be like a fish out of water
- black sheep (of the family)
- call a spade a spade
- call it a day
- come under fire
- cost an arm and a leg
- cry wolf
- do the trick
- face the music
- gain ground
- get into deep water
- hit the nail on the head

- (not) hold water
- keep an eye on something/someone
- keep your head above water
- make waves
- not have a leg to stand on
- old wives' tale
- out of the blue
- pain in the neck
- pass the buck
- pull somebody's leg
- rack one's brain(s)
- spill the beans
- take your hat off to somebody
- throw in the towel
- trick of the trade
- under a cloud
- until you are blue in the face

 Teaching tip

Some coursebooks teach idioms by showing, or asking students to draw, a picture showing their literal meaning: for example, showing a hammer striking a nail to illustrate 'hit the nail on the head'. This is tempting, but not actually very helpful. What students need to know is the actual communicative message of the idiom; making them focus on the concrete image used may confuse, unless the metaphor is 'transparent'.

1.3.7 Meanings of phrasal verbs

Outline	Students use the base meanings of prepositions or adverbs added to verbs in order to create and understand new multi-word verbs.
Focus	Meanings of prepositions and adverbs used in prepositional and phrasal verbs
Age	Adolescent–Adult
Level	Intermediate
Time	30 minutes
Preparation	A list of prepositions and adverbs that appear in phrasal verbs, with their meanings, copied for students; see *Boxes 1.3.7a* and *b;* dictionaries, paper or digital

Procedure

1 Give out the list of prepositions and adverbs used in phrasal verbs in *Box 1.3.7a*, and teach all the ones which the students may not know.
2 Invite students to tell you a few of the two- (or three-) word verbs they already know which use these items.
3 Give out a list of verbs which might go with any of the items you have just studied and invite students to create new verbs by combining them. See *Box 1.3.7b*. The condition is that these new verbs must NOT be ones they are already familiar with.
4 Students work in pairs and try to reach at least seven new verbs. By each verb they must put a definition (or L1 translation) and a sentence contextualizing it.
5 They use dictionaries to check if these verbs really exist, and if they have the meanings they expected.
6 Take in the lists, and in a later lesson teach or review all the verbs that students created and which do indeed exist.

Variation

Copy the lists of verbs, prepositions and adverbs onto stiff paper and cut them up into single-word cards. Groups of students can be given sets of these and asked to create as many phrasal verb combinations as they can in five minutes.

Box 1.3.7a: Meanings of phrasal verbs

Prepositions and adverbs used with phrasal verbs

Meanings that are concrete and obvious:

- about
- in
- over
- away
- off
- round
- back
- on
- up
- down
- out
- with

Some possible meanings that are figurative and may not be obvious:

- away = stored (for example, in a drawer or cupboard)
- off = not working, not activated
- on = working, activated
- over = from one side to another
- up = completely, absolutely, or more loudly

From *Vocabulary Activites* © Cambridge University Press 2012   PHOTOCOPIABLE

Box 1.3.7b: Meanings of phrasal verbs

One-word verbs to be made into two-word ones

- break
- go
- put
- bring
- hold
- set
- carry
- look
- sit
- come
- make
- take
- find
- move
- turn
- get
- pick
- work
- give
- point

1.3.8 Find a one-word verb that means the same!

Outline	Students compete to find as many single-word verbs they can that correspond to given phrasal or prepositional verbs.
Focus	Phrasal or prepositional verbs
Age	Adolescent–Adult
Level	Advanced
Time	20–30 minutes
Preparation	List of two-word verbs that have one-word equivalents; *Box 1.3.8* copied for students; optionally, monolingual English dictionaries or thesauri

Procedure

1 Tell students they will get a list of phrasal or prepositional verbs, and have to find for each a single-word verb that means the same. They should find as many as they can in fifteen minutes. They may use dictionaries or thesauri.

2 Divide the class into groups of about four or five students, and give them each the list from *Box 1.3.8*. Tell each group to elect a secretary who will fill in the verbs, helped by other group members.

3 Stop the process after ten minutes (or whenever you feel that most of the groups have found as many as they can), and tell or show the class the answers (see *Answers (Box 1.3.8)*. Each group ticks off its correct answers and works out how many it got right. Alternatively, take in the papers and check them yourself while the class gets on with some individual work.

4 Announce the winners!

5 Review or teach the verbs which not all the groups knew, or which they found only by looking them up.

Follow-up

Ask the students in pairs to compose a short text using four or five of the phrasal verbs we've looked at. They then exchange with another pair, who 'translate' the passage into a text with one-word verbs. Note how formal the text has now become!

 Teaching tip

When giving a group task, particularly if it is a group competition, remember to tell the class in advance how long they have to do it, and how you are going to stop them. It's a good idea to have a bell available, as a stopping signal.

Box 1.3.8: Find a one-word verb that means the same!

1 back up ....
2 break down ....
3 come across ....
4 come back ....
5 come together ....
6 consist of ....
7 get up ....
8 give back ....
9 give up, give in ....
10 go/turn around ....
11 go away ....
12 go down ....
13 go up ....
14 let down ....

15 make up (a story) ....
16 pile up ....
17 put off (to another time) ....
18 put out (a fire) ....
19 run away ....
20 set up ....
21 sort out ....
22 speak to ....
23 take apart ....
24 take away ....
25 talk about ....
26 throw away ....
27 wait for ....
28 work together ....

From *Vocabulary Activities* © Cambridge University Press 2012   PHOTOCOPIABLE

Answers (Box 1.3.8 Find a one-word verb that means the same!)

1 support
2 collapse
3 encounter
4 return
5 congregate
6 comprise
7 rise
8 return (an object)
9 surrender
10 return (intransitive)

11 depart
12 descend
13 ascend, mount
14 disappoint
15 compose
16 accumulate
17 postpone
18 extinguish
19 flee
20 establish

21 classify, solve
22 address
23 dismantle
24 remove
25 discuss
26 discard
27 await
28 collaborate

1.3.9 Book, play or movie titles

Outline	Students discuss titles of books, plays and movies they know.
Focus	Clichés and quotations
Age	Adolescent–Adult
Level	Advanced
Time	20 minutes
Preparation	A set of English-language movie, play or book titles, displayed on the board or copied for students; use *Box 1.3.9* or compile your own

Procedure

1   Show the students a list of English-language movie, play or book titles (use *Box 1.3.9*, or your own list, or a combination). Invite them to add more; but tell them that titles they suggest must not have proper nouns.

2   Select the titles you think will interest students, and discuss: Do they understand the meanings and perhaps implications? (Some are based on double meanings.) Teach the proverbs, quotations and clichés from which they are taken.

3   If most of the students are acquainted with the movie, play or book in question, discuss the point of the title for each: what is its relevance to the content of the work itself?

Box 1.3.9: Book, play or movie titles

1 *All good things*	11 *Ice age*
2 *All that jazz*	12 *Lilies of the field*
3 *All the king's men*	13 *Look who's talking*
4 *All's well that ends well*	14 *Much ado about nothing*
5 *An officer and a gentleman*	15 *Pulp fiction*
6 *As good as it gets*	16 *The grapes of wrath*
7 *Consider her ways*	17 *The paper chase*
8 *For your eyes only*	18 *The sixth sense*
9 *Gone with the wind*	19 *The ten commandments*
10 *Great expectations*	20 *Walk the line*

From *Vocabulary Activities* © Cambridge University Press 2012   PHOTOCOPIABLE

Acknowledgement

Adapted from an idea in Scott Thornbury's book *How to Teach Vocabulary* (see *References and further reading*).

1.3.10 Creating compound nouns

Outline	Students create compound nouns from a pool of simple nouns.
Focus	Compound nouns
Age	Pre-adolescent–Adult
Level	Intermediate–Advanced
Time	10–15 minutes
Preparation	Use *Box 1.3.10*, copied for students or displayed on the board

Procedure

1   Show the students how one of the nouns in the list can be combined with another to make a compound noun: for example, *a business school*, meaning a school that teaches subjects to do with business.
2   Invite them to suggest other combinations, and say what they mean. Note that sometimes two words may be hyphenated, as in *apple-tree*.
3   In pairs or small groups, students continue to think up further combinations and write them down. For each, they have to say (but not write) what it means.
4   Elicit some of the resulting ideas.

Note

Remind students that even when the first noun of the combination relates to a lot of things, it is normally in the singular: so a shop that sells shoes is a *shoe* (not 'shoes') *shop*. Many other languages use a plural in such combinations, which can lead to mistakes in English.

Variations

1   Add to the list, or substitute, nouns you have recently taught.
2   Invite students to take one of the items, and create further combinations that use it with any other noun they wish, not from the list. If it is *apple*, for example, they might suggest:
     an apple pie, an apple core, an apple seed, an apple basket.
3   Challenge students to create further combinations whose meaning is something that doesn't in fact exist or is very unlikely, for example, *an apple language* meaning the language spoken by apples, *a book tree*, meaning a tree on which books grow.

Box 1.3.10: Creating compound nouns

Intermediate

- apple
- book
- box
- business
- club

- container
- computer
- game
- language
- room

- school
- shoe
- shop
- sports
- tree

Advanced

- adult
- author
- authority
- code
- colleague
- community
- constraint
- export

- factor
- labour
- legislation
- method
- paradigm
- period
- project
- research

- section
- shift
- source
- summary
- text
- tradition
- university

From *Vocabulary Activities* © Cambridge University Press 2012   PHOTOCOPIABLE

1.4 BUILDING ON WORD STRUCTURE

In this section students learn new words by focusing on their morphological structure.

1.4.1 Suffixes for parts of speech

Outline	Students brainstorm words that end with particular suffixes.
Focus	Suffixes typical of specific parts of speech
Age	Adolescent–Adult
Level	Intermediate –advanced
Time	20–30 minutes
Preparation	The table shown in *Box 1.4.1a*, copied for students

Procedure

1 Distribute the table and talk students through the information given.
2 Invite students to think of as many other examples as they can of words which end in each suffix shown .
3 Using the extra examples provided by students, add to your original table, enlarge, and post on the classroom wall for future reference.

Follow-ups

1 Encourage students to notice further examples of such suffixes that they may come across in their reading.
2 If students have a corpus available with a concordancing tool (see, for example, http://corpus.byu.edu/bnc/), they can feed in a suffix prefixed by a * (for example, *tion*) to get a large number of sample words.

Variation

Provide students with the list of base words in *Box 1.4.1b*, and challenge them to transform the words into another part of speech using an appropriate suffix. Warn students that sometimes the end of the original word might need to be changed a little, as well as adding a suffix; for example:

> nature → natural
> obstinate → obstinacy.

If they don't know which the suffix is, they should look it up in a dictionary. (But note that many words with such suffixes do not have a root which functions normally as a separate word; examples are *portable, function*.)

Notes

1   Students will notice that some of the words with typical suffixes for one part of speech may sometimes be used as another; for example, the word *native*, originally an adjective, is often used as a noun. See *1.2.12 Same word, different part of speech(1)*.

2   The suffixes shown here do not have any very marked meaning apart from showing the 'verbiness' or 'nouniness', etc. of an item. For prefixes and suffixes that have specific meanings, see *1.4.3 Find a new word*.

3   The suffix *-ize* is conventionally classified as an American suffix, and *-ise* as British. But in fact *-ize* is used quite commonly in Britain and worldwide in words like *organize, realize*; so tell your students that if they aren't sure, they should use the *z*. Exceptions include *surprise, advertise, advise* which they should spell with an *s*.

♀ Teaching tip

When teaching students new vocabulary, you will usually have prepared a set of items you intend to cover. But remember always to invite students to add more: anything they happen to know that is connected to the same area. This not only increases vocabulary learning, it also contributes to a positive classroom climate of teacher–student cooperation.

Box 1.4.1a: Suffixes for parts of speech

Part of speech	Suffix	Examples
Nouns	-ment	apartment, ...
	-age	baggage, ...
	-ery, -ary	bakery, ...
	-ity	community, ...
	-ence	existence, ...
	-ship	friendship, ...
	-tion	function, ...
	-ance	importance, ...
	-ness	kindness, ...
	-hood	motherhood, ...
	-sion	possession, ...
Verbs	-ify	beautify, ...
	-en	freshen, ...
	-ize/-ise	realize/ise, ...
	-ate	tolerate, ...
Adjectives	-ful	careful, ...
	-ic	comic, ...
	-ous	dangerous, ...
	-ish	foolish, ...
	-y	funny, ...
	-ant	ignorant, ...
	-ent	independent, ...
	-al	natural, ...
	-ive	passive, ...
Adverbs	-ly	quickly, ...

From *Vocabulary Activities* © Cambridge University Press 2012   PHOTOCOPIABLE

Box 1.4.1b: Suffixes for parts of speech

Verb form	Noun form	Adjective form	Verb form
annoy		active	
assist		beautiful	
attract		civil	
create		different	
describe		diverse	
frequent		light	
inject		live	
instruct		special	
relax		simple	
vacate		solid	
		terrified	
Noun form	**Adjective form**	**Adjective form**	**Adverb form**
drama		actual	
effect		certain	
fame		civil	
industry		comfortable	
music		convenient	
nation		funny	
logic		hesitant	
region		obvious	
science		possible	
sun		particular	
		polite	
		precise	
		private	
		significant	
		slight	
		total	

1.4.2 Exploring affixes

Outline	Students find words that have given prefixes (and suffixes), and work out the meanings of the affixes.
Focus	Prefixes (and suffixes: see *Variation*)
Age	Adolescent–Adult
Level	Intermediate–Advanced
Time	20–30 minutes
Preparation	Sets of five words, each beginning with a different prefix underlined; see *Box 1.4.2a* for some suggested words or come up with your own. Each word in the group is written at the head of a blank sheet of paper. Make several copies of each sheet, so that all pairs of students can be working on one of them simultaneously, with at least one of each in reserve.

Procedure

1 Check that students know what a prefix is, and provide an example showing how it changes the meaning of the word it is attached to. For example:

   misuse   subconscious.

2 Give each pair of students one of the sheets you have prepared. Leave the rest in a reserve pile on your desk, or in another central accessible area in the classroom.

3 Tell students to write on the sheet as many other words beginning with the underlined prefix shown in the word at the top of the page as they can. They should also write, at the bottom of the page, what they know, or think, the meaning of the prefix to be.

4 When each pair has finished, they return the sheet to the reserve pile and take another.

5 If the second sheet has already been worked on by another pair of students, the next pair first check the definition at the bottom of the page and change it if they think it is wrong. Then they add any further words they can think of to the list above.

6 When the first pair has finished all five sheets, stop everyone and check the results. Add to any of the lists any more words you feel it would be useful for students to know.

Vocabulary Activities

Variation

Do the same activity using suffixes. See *Box 1.4.2b.*

You may want, in the course of this activity, to draw students' attention to the spelling and pronunciation rules of the prefixes *in-* and *con-*: that they become *im-* and *com-* before the letters *m,b,p*; *il-* and *col-* before *l*; and *ir-* and *cor-* before *r*.

Follow-ups

1 Tell students to use their dictionaries to find at least one more word for each prefix for homework, and bring it to the next lesson to teach the rest of the class.
2 *1.4.3 Find a new word* is a good follow-up to this activity

Notes

1 Some of the words which include affixes may have in fact lost any obvious connection with the root meaning of the affix; for example, *subject*, as in 'the subject of the sentence' has no obvious connection with the 'under' meaning of *sub*. You'll need to make students aware of this: but within the list of words they find, there should be enough samples which are obviously connected to the original meaning of the affix to enable them to identify it.
2 Occasionally a prefix may have two distinct meanings; for example, *in-* can mean 'not' or (less commonly) 'in'; *ex-* can mean 'out (of)' or (normally with a hyphen) 'former'. When students are working on one of these, make them aware of the possible confusion, and tell them to keep to the meaning shown in the original word.

♀ Teaching tips

It's always a problem to know when to stop a group or pair activity when students are naturally working at different speeds, and some finish before others. Two good tips are:

1 Stop the activity when the first group or pair finishes; but remember to warn the class in advance that this is what you are going to do, to prevent protests by those who haven't finished.
2 Make sure you prepare a reserve activity for those who finish early. It might be thinking up more items similar to those they've been working on, or finding more in a dictionary, or just getting on with homework. Whatever it is, make sure it is built in to the initial instructions, so that students know what to do if they finish and other students are still working.

Box 1.4.2a: Exploring affixes

Prefixes: Intermediate

- <u>coll</u>aborate
- <u>com</u>panion
- <u>con</u>front
- <u>cor</u>respond
- <u>dis</u>please
- <u>down</u>size
- <u>ex</u>-wife

- <u>ex</u>it
- <u>im</u>possible
- <u>il</u>legal
- <u>in</u>definite
- <u>in</u>doors
- <u>inter</u>face
- <u>ir</u>responsible

- <u>mega</u>ton
- <u>micro</u>wave
- <u>mini</u>mize
- <u>re</u>view
- <u>trans</u>atlantic
- <u>un</u>happy

Prefixes: Advanced

- <u>a</u>moral
- <u>anti</u>septic
- <u>auto</u>matic
- <u>counter</u>attack
- <u>cyber</u>space

- <u>de</u>forest
- <u>e</u>mail
- <u>mono</u>logue
- <u>non</u>-existent
- <u>out</u>play

- <u>over</u>do
- <u>post</u>dated
- <u>phil</u>anthropy
- <u>pre</u>arrange
- <u>pro</u>pose

- <u>semi</u>-final
- <u>sub</u>way
- <u>tele</u>communications
- <u>under</u>line
- <u>up</u>grade

Box 1.4.2b: Exploring affixes

Suffixes: Intermediate

- care<u>less</u>
- do<u>able</u>/vis<u>ible</u>
- inform<u>er</u>/direct<u>or</u>
- psycho<u>logy</u>
- violin<u>ist</u>

Suffixes: Advanced

- employ<u>ee</u>
- claustro<u>phobia</u>
- princ<u>ess</u>
- social<u>ism</u>
- solv<u>ent</u>

1.4.3 Find a new word

Outline	Students find new words using prefixes and suffixes.
Focus	Prefixes and suffixes
Age	Adolescent–Adult
Level	Intermediate–Advanced
Time	Ten minutes
Preparation	Dictionaries; lists of prefixes and suffixes such as those in *Box 1.4.3*

Procedure

1 Write two headings on the board, *Prefixes* and *Suffixes*, and write a set of about ten of each type of affix under them.
2 Check that students understand all the meanings of the affixes.
3 Tell them that they have 15 minutes to find out from their dictionaries or from online sources words that they didn't know before that use these affixes.
4 After 15 minutes, tell students to join together in groups of four and share their findings.
5 Each group then presents its new words to the rest of the class; you may need to help with explanations.

Notes

1 This is a good follow-up to either *1.4.2 Exploring affixes* or *1.4.1 Suffixes for parts of speech*.
2 It is, of course, impossible to use a conventional paper dictionary to look up words that end with a particular suffix! But if the students have online computers or mobile phones with Internet then they can use a corpus website as suggested in a *Follow-up* to 1.4.1. Or they can consult more advanced English speakers – or you!

Follow-up

From the words the students have found, select those you feel are most useful, note them down and do later review activities on them to make sure they are remembered.

Box 1.4.3: Find a new word

Prefixes

Intermediate

- re-
- mini-
- un-
- trans-
- mis-
- ex-
- dis-
- mega-
- in-, ir-, il- (=not)
- micro-
- down-
- con-, com-, cor-, col-
- inter-
- in-, ir-, il- (=inside)

Advanced

- e-
- up-
- a-
- mono-
- auto-
- phil-
- cyber-
- pro-
- non-
- anti-
- sub-
- post-
- tele-
- counter-
- semi-
- out-
- de-
- over-
- pre-
- under-

Suffixes

Intermediate

- -less
- -ate
- -able/-ible
- -ly
- -er/-or
- -ive
- -ology
- -al
- -ist
- -y
- -ment
- -ful
- -tion
- -sion
- -ance/-ence
- -ness
- -ize/-ise

Advanced

- -ee
- -ism
- -phobia
- -en/-ant (adj.)
- -ent (n.)
- -ess
- -hood
- -ship
- -ery, ary
- -ify
- -en
- -age
- -ic
- -ish
- -ous
- -ity

1.4.4 Word families

Outline	Students complete tables of word families: nouns, verbs, adjectives and adverbs.
Focus	Nouns, verbs, adjectives and adverbs derived from a common root
Age	Adolescent–Adult
Level	Advanced
Time	15–20 minutes
Preparation	Empty tables such as that shown in *Box 1.4.4*, copied for students; or students can simply draw their own; dictionaries

Procedure

1   Draw a table like that shown in *Box 1.4.4* on the board, and fill in a word that you know has corresponding words in other parts of speech; for example, *ignorant*.

Noun	Verb	Adjective	Adverb
		ignorant	

2   Then, with the help of the students, fill in the other columns, as follows:

Noun	Verb	Adjective	Adverb
ignorance	ignore	ignorant	ignorantly

Sometimes the word may not have corresponding items to fill all the columns; for example:

Noun	Verb	Adjective	Adverb
importance	–	important	importantly

3   Select a few words from those you have taught recently (which you are aware have at least one other corresponding word in another part of speech) and write them up in the appropriate spaces.

4   Challenge students to fill in the columns, reassuring them that occasionally one or two spaces may be left empty. They may refer to dictionaries as necessary.

5   Check in full class. Note that occasionally there may be more than one possibility for a particular part of speech.

Follow-ups

1 Invite students to pick out words from a text they are reading that might be used as *base* words to fill in further rows of items.

2 Do the same occasionally in later lessons with new items – from a reading text, for example – that have similar *families*.

3 Ask students in pairs to prepare for each other gapfill exercises on word roots and derivations of the type:

Despite her strong .... , I didn't believe her. (DENY)

Let them work for 15 or 20 minutes preparing their exercises. Then they exchange, do the exercises, and correct or help each other as necessary.

Notes

1 If students have done *1.4.1 Suffixes for parts of speech*, tell them to refer back to the suffixes they learnt there: they may be useful for this task.

2 Sometimes words are spelt the same even if they are used in other parts of speech (see *1.2.12 Same word, different part of speech (1)* and *1.2.13 Same word, different part of speech (2)*). They may, however, be pronounced differently; see the *Notes* at the end of the first of these two activities.

Box 1.4.4: Word families

Noun	Verb	Adjective	Adverb

From *Vocabulary Activities* © Cambridge University Press 2012   PHOTOCOPIABLE

1.4.5 From Greek and Latin (1)

Outline	Students learn some useful Greek and Latin nouns used in English and their plurals.
Focus	Greek and Latin nouns
Age	Adolescent–Adult
Level	Advanced
Time	30–40 minutes
Preparation	A selection from the list of singular nouns shown in *Box 1.4.5*, displayed on the board or copied for students; use as many as you think your class can cope with in one lesson

Procedure

1 Ask the students which of the words they know the meaning of, and if they know any of their plural forms.

2 Approve or correct; then add information about the rest of the nouns in the list: their meanings and plurals.

3 Tell the students that their homework is to look for sentence contexts for as many of the words as they can. They may simply Google™ them; or they may look at one of the corpus-based websites suggested on p. 45.

4 In the following lesson, share some of the sentences that the students have found.

Note

This activity is particularly appropriate for academic classes, as these words are most common in academic discourse.

 Teaching tip

Even if you intend to go through an exercise with the full class, it is usually worth getting students to do it on their own first, either individually or in pairs. That way you make sure that everyone engages with the task, and the full-class process goes much faster.

Box 1.4.5: From Greek and Latin (1)

Singular nouns

- addendum
- automaton
- axis
- cactus
- census
- corpus
- crisis
- criterion
- dogma
- encyclopedia (encyclopaedia)
- erratum
- focus
- formula
- forum
- fungus
- genus
- medium
- millenium
- phenomenon
- prospectus
- radius
- schema
- series
- species
- stigma
- syllabus
- terminus
- uterus
- virus
- vortex

Singular and plural nouns

- addendum (pl. addenda)
- automaton (pl. automata)
- axis (pl.axes)
- cactus (pl. cactus/cacti)
- census (pl. censuses)
- corpus (pl. corpora)
- crisis (pl.crises)
- criterion (pl. criteria)
- dogma (pl. dogmata/dogmas)
- encyclopedia (pl. encyclopedias)
- erratum (pl. errata)
- focus (pl. foci/focuses)
- formula (pl. formulae)
- forum (pl. fora/forums)
- fungus (pl. fungi)
- genus (pl. genera)
- medium (pl. media)
- millenium (pl. millenia)
- phenomenon (pl. phenomena)
- prospectus (pl. prospecti/ prospectuses)
- radius (pl. radii)
- schema (pl. schemata/schemas)
- series (pl. series)
- species (pl. species)
- stigma (pl. stigmata/stigmas)
- syllabus (pl. syllabi/syllabuses)
- terminus (pl. termini/terminuses)
- uterus (pl. uteri/uteruses)
- virus (pl. viruses)
- vortex (pl. vortices)

1.4.6 From Greek and Latin (2)

Outline	Students learn the meanings of some Greek and Latin roots, and apply them to English words.
Focus	Greek and Latin word roots
Age	Adolescent–Adult
Level	Advanced
Time	30–40 minutes
Preparation	A selection of items from the list shown in *Box 1.4.6*, displayed on the board or copied for students; computers with internet access

Procedure

1 Distribute the lists of items to students or display them on the board.

2 Go through them and discuss each: do they know any words – in English or in their mother tongue – that include them?

3 Teach or elicit the root meaning of each item.

4 Tell students to go to their computers and look up the roots on a corpus (for example, the *British National Corpus* on http://corpus.byu.edu/bnc/). Usually if you enter an asterisk immediately before and after the root (for example: *anthropo*) you will be shown all the words that include it that are in the corpus.

5 For each root students should list words they knew before, as well as at least one new word they learnt from their research. They should make sure they know the meaning of any new words (check a dictionary).

6 They then come back to full class and share findings.

Variation

Single items can also serve as a basis for *1.1.2 Word of the day*. In this case, simply teach the root and associated words, without sending students to look it up.

Notes

1 Students who speak a Latin-based language such as Spanish are likely to be familiar with many words based on these roots. Others will know some of them because they are used in international academic terminology.

2 Note that in any given text, most of the words are likely to be Germanic, and only a minority of Latin or Greek origin. The proportion of Latin or Greek words, however, rises substantially in more formal and/or academic

passages. If you type any text into *VocabProfile* (http://www.lextutor.ca/ freq/eng/), the resulting analysis will show you the proportion of Greek- or Latin-origin words as compared to Germanic.

Follow-up

More academic students might be interested to find further information, or check out which of the items are in fact from Latin and which Greek, using an etymological dictionary, or the *Online Etymology Dictionary* at http:// www.etymonline.com/.

 Teaching tip

Whenever a word has some kind of irregular grammatical form (an unusual plural, for nouns, or an irregular past, for verbs) it's a good idea to teach it at the same time as you teach the base form of the word itself, rather than later.

Box 1.4.6: From Greek and Latin (2)

- *anthropo* (man)
- *audi* (listen/hear)
- *cosm* (universe)
- *dict* (say)
- *duc, duct* (lead)
- *form* (form, image)
- *geo* (earth)
- *graph* (write)
- *homo* (same)
- *leg, lect* (read)
- *log* (word)
- *manu* (hand)
- *medi* (middle)

- *pan* (all)
- *path* (feel)
- *plen* (full)
- *port* (carry)
- *pluri* (many)
- *multi* (many)
- *scrib, script* (write)
- *sent, sens* (feel)
- *sequ* (follow)
- *soci* (friend)
- *spic, spect* (look)
- *vid, vis* (see)

1.5 NAMES

This section provides activities that teach or practise proper names in English: personal names, names of countries, nationalities, languages, months and days of the week.

1.5.1 What would you like to be called?

Outline	Students choose an English name they might like for themselves.
Focus	Common personal first names; pronunciation and spelling
Age	Young–Pre-adolescent
Level	Beginner
Time	10–15 minutes
Preparation	A list of popular English first names as shown in *Box 1.5.1* (or a selection from it), copied for students; or download your own updated list from an online list of popular first names: see *Note* below

Procedure

1 Distribute the list of names (or a shorter selection from it for younger or less advanced students).
2 Ask students to tick off those names they are familiar with.
3 Ask them which names were left. Encourage them to ask you if they aren't sure how to pronounce any name and help them to pronounce it correctly.
4 Ask them: if they were able to choose an English name of their own, which would it be? And why? Allow them to choose a name they know even if it is not on the list.
5 Invite students to walk round the classroom asking each other *What's your name?* and answering with their chosen name.
6 Students return to their places. Challenge them to recall each other's new names: *His name is Benjamin! Her name is Charlotte!*
7 Write up the chosen names on the board, and draw students' attention to their spelling.

Variations

1 Students look for names in their own language which have counterparts in English. Can they identify any consistent differences of spelling and pronunciation?

2 After looking at and discussing a few English names from the list, students take their own (real) first names and discuss whether these would be easy or difficult for speakers of other languages with whom they might communicate in English. How might they be pronounced with an English accent? (Such adaptations can be very amusing!)

3 Ask students how they might adapt their own names to make them easier to cope with internationally. Would they choose an English name equivalent? Or just 'tweak' the spelling or pronunciation of their own name to make it easier?

4 Use the phonetically spelt names, such as *Anna, Justin* and *Daniel*, as bases for very easy reading (decoding) practice or dictation.

Follow-ups

1 Ask which English names – whether from the list or not – students have come across: in their reading, or perhaps people they know, or celebrities.

2 Invite students to find out the meaning of the name they chose on the Internet. (Have a look at *Behindthename* http://www.behindthename.com/.)

3 Ask students if they would like to continue to use their 'English' names in English lessons: if so, continue to address them by these names.

Note

For more names that are currently popular in English-speaking countries, look at http://www.babynames.co.uk/(UK) or www.babynames.com/Names/Popular/(USA).

♀ Teaching tip

Don't worry about the political correctness of suggesting that students choose a name other than their own for this activity or even beyond it (*Follow-up 3*). Students don't see it as implying a threat to their own cultural and national identity! In my experience they usually – particularly the younger ones – enjoy it as kind of game or role-play. (And for those who happen to dislike their given name, it's a welcome opportunity to escape it!)

Box 1.5.1: What would you like to be called?

Girls' names	Boys' names
• Abigail	• Aaron
• Alexandra	• Adam
• Anna	• Alexander
• Amber	• Andrew
• Bethany	• Anthony
• Brianna	• Benjamin
• Charlotte	• Cameron
• Chloe	• Connor
• Courtney	• Daniel
• Elizabeth	• David
• Emily	• Dylan
• Emma	• Ethan
• Georgia	• George
• Grace	• Jack
• Hannah	• Jacob
• Isabella	• James
• Jasmine	• John
• Jessica	• Jordan
• Lauren	• Joseph
• Lucy	• Joshua
• Madeline	• Justin
• Maria	• Luke
• Megan	• Matthew
• Nicole	• Michael
• Olivia	• Nathan
• Rachel	• Robert
• Rebecca	• Ryan
• Sarah	• Samuel
• Sophie	• Thomas
• Stephanie	• William

1.5.2 Putting it on the map

Outline	Students write in names of countries on maps.
Focus	Names of countries
Age	Young–Adolescent
Level	Beginner–Intermediate
Time	15 minutes
Preparation	Blank maps of the world, as shown in *Box 1.5.2*, or download from the Internet; make copies for students, enlarged to fill an A4 page, and have one big copy displayed on the board

Procedure

1 Distribute the maps, and tell students to write in the name of their own country or countries (in English!) in the appropriate place. Add it/them to the map on the board.

2 Each student writes on their map the name of three more countries they know how to say in English.

3 Students come up to the board to write in the names of more countries (the ones they have noted on their own maps) (see *Teaching Tip* in *1.3.3, Identifying lexical phrases*). Correct spelling as necessary. As they do so, the other students copy from the board any country names they had not yet filled in on their own maps.

4 Add another five countries you think it would be useful for students to know – perhaps ones that have been in the news recently – and teach their English spelling and pronunciation.

5 Tell students to staple or paste the folded map into their vocabulary notebooks for future reference.

Variation

Have a brief discussion in class, perhaps in L1, about the English names of countries compared to their names in the students' L1. Are there any which are completely different? Where they are very similar, draw students' attention to regular changes in the transformation from one language to another, in spelling or pronunciation.

Follow-ups

1 In later lessons, add further country names whenever these are mentioned in the news.

2 Use the opportunity to teach and use the names of the nationalities (*British, Chinese*, etc.): see the next activity *1.5.3 Nations: what are they good at?*

Box 1.5.2: Putting it on the map

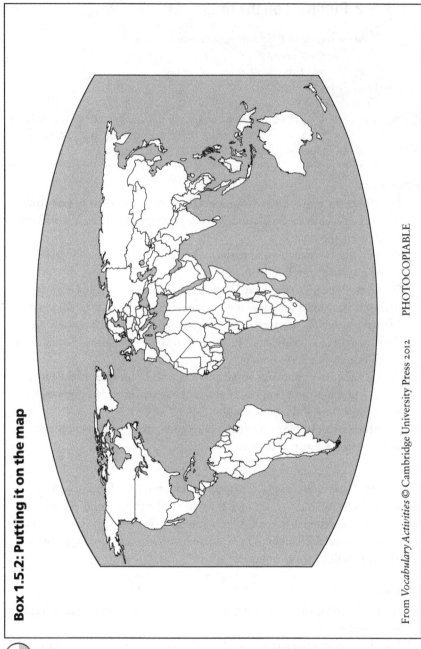

1.5.3 Nations: what are they good at?

Outline	Students discuss what each nation is perceived by many people to be good at.
Focus	Names for people of different nationalities
Age	Adolescent–Adult
Level	Beginner–Intermediate
Time	20 minutes
Preparation	*Box 1.5.3* (provided to give you some examples, not for student use)

Procedure

1 Ask students what the names are of people who live in different countries bordering on, or near to, their own country. As they suggest them, add them to lists on the board, sorting them under headings like those shown in *Box 1.5.3*.

2 Draw their attention to the different sets of names: particularly the first column. Adjectival nouns which are often (but not always) the name of a language are usually prefixed with *the* and function as plurals:

    The French are . . .

3 Invite students to add a few more names of nationalities they know from other parts of the world; stop when you have twenty or thirty on the board.

4 Tell students to discuss in groups the national stereotypes of some of the groups shown on the board: what are they supposed to be good at? What is special about them, according to the stereotype?

5 Share ideas, and discuss how true they think these stereotypes are. Like many stereotypes, there may be some truth in them; or there may not.

Variation

Ask students what they think the stereotypes are of their own nationality in the eyes of others. How true are they?

Note

Stereotyping is a fact of life, and isn't necessarily bad: there are sometimes factual bases to generalizations about groups of people, which can be informative and helpful – provided they are recognized as generalizations, not overall truths applied unthinkingly to individuals.

Teaching tip

For schoolteachers: when you get into controversial issues like this one, it may be worth spending a few minutes discussing them in L1 if the class is not up to an English discussion at this level. You don't need to feel guilty about it: the educational value arguably outweighs the disadvantage of loss of 'English-speaking' time.

Box 1.5.3: Nations: what are they good at?

Adjectival nouns with *the*	Plural nouns ending in *-an*	Short plurals	Plural nouns ending in *-i*
the British	Algerians	Arabs	Iraqis
the Chinese	Americans	Danes	Israelis
the English	Angolans	Finns	Kuwaitis
the French	Argentinians	Greeks	Nepalis
the Irish	Australians	Poles	Pakistanis
the Japanese	Austrians	Scots	
the Lebanese	Belgians	Slavs	
the Maltese	Brazilians	Swedes	
the Portuguese	Canadians		
the Swiss	Chileans		
	Egyptians		
	Germans		
	Hungarians		
	Indians		
	Iranians		
	Italians		
	Jordanians		
	Kenyans		
	Koreans		
	Mexicans		
	Palestinians		
	Russians		
	Serbians		

1.5.4 How many languages do we speak between us?

Outline	Students find out what languages are spoken by their classmates and families.
Focus	Names of languages
Age	Young–Adolescent
Level	Beginner–Intermediate
Time	10–15 minutes
Preparation	A list of endings to the names of languages, such as those in *Box 1.5.4*

Procedure

1 Divide the board into two sections, headed *Languages we speak, Languages our families speak*.
2 Invite students to tell you which languages they speak.
3 Now invite students to add any more that are spoken by their parents or other members of their families, and write them up under the appropriate heading. Again, teach the English names for these languages as necessary. How many languages have you now reached?
4 Draw attention to the different kinds of endings to the names of languages, and which (endings) are the most common (perhaps using *Box 1.5.4*).

Follow-ups

1 Add another heading *Languages we'd like to speak* and invite students to contribute any other languages they might like to learn to speak in the future, and why.
2 Go back to the list of nationalities you worked on in *1.5.3 Nations: what are they good at?*, or countries on the map in *1.5.2 Putting it on the map*, and discuss with students what languages are spoken by the different peoples or in the different countries.

Box 1.5.4: How many languages do we speak between us?

-ish	-ese	-i	-ic	-an	other
English	Burmese	Bengali	Arabic	Catalan	Basque
Polish	Chinese	Gujerati	Icelandic	German	Czech
Spanish	Japanese	Hindi	Amharic	Hungarian	Dutch
Turkish	Javanese	Punjabi		Italian	French
	Portuguese	Nepali		Russian	Greek
	Vietnamese			Slovakian	Malay
					Tamil

1.5.5 Special dates

Outline	Students discuss the significance of special dates.
Focus	Months of the year, dates and days of the week (see *Variation*)
Age	Young–Adolescent
Level	Beginner
Time	20 minutes
Preparation	*Box 1.5.5* (provided for your reference, not for student use)

Procedure

1 Review with students how we express dates in writing and in speech: there's a difference (see *Box 1.5.5*).
2 Tell each student to write down a date (day, month, year) that is special for them, for any reason.
3 Students find partners, tell each other their dates and spend three minutes trying to guess what the significance is of their partner's date. If they find out, they continue to tell each other about the background to their dates.
4 At the end of three minutes, stop the interaction: anyone whose date has not been guessed tells their partner the answer.
5 They then do the same with another partner.
6 After two or three such 'rounds', bring the class back to their own seats and invite some of the students to share with the full class their special dates and the background to them.

Variation

Do the same with days of the week. The reason could be because of a particular event that fell (or will fall) on that day, or because of a routine event that happens every week.

 Teaching tip

If students just learn the days of the week as a chant (*Sunday Monday Tuesday . . .*), they will be unable easily to name or identify any single day on its own without mumbling through the entire sequence; and even then they risk getting it wrong. It is important to provide them with opportunities to encounter and use each word as representing an individual meaning of its own, independent of the others. The same goes for basic numbers and months of the year.

Box 1.5.5: Special dates

There are a lot of variations, but these are the predominant forms:

Dates in writing

- Dates in words in most of the countries of the world: December 20 2012
- Dates in words in the USA: December 20, 2012
- Dates in numbers in most of the countries of the world: 20/12/12 or 20.12.12
- Dates in numbers in the USA: 12/20/12 or 12.20.12
- Note that it is rare these days to insert ordinal numbers like 1st or 3rd in writing dates.

Dates in speech

- In most countries of the world: December the twentieth, two thousand and twelve or twenty-twelve
- In the USA: December twentieth, twenty-twelve.

From *Vocabulary Activities* © Cambridge University Press 2012   PHOTOCOPIABLE

2 Vocabulary review

The activities in this section provide ideas for re-encounter and practice of vocabulary previously taught. A single encounter with a new vocabulary item may be virtually useless: it is likely to be forgotten if the learner is not reminded of it soon after; and research indicates that learners need about ten to sixteen re-encounters with a new item in order for it to become part of their active vocabulary (see reference to multiple encounters under *Vocabulary teaching* section in *Guidelines*). Review activities also deepen and enrich students' awareness of meanings, collocations, connotations, alternative spellings and pronunciations and so on.

2.1 SINGLE ITEMS

It is often helpful, particularly at the early stages of learning new vocabulary, to focus on and practise each newly learnt word or expression in isolation, as well as in wider contexts. This section provides ideas for review of single items.

2.1.1 Listing from memory

Outline	Students recall as many as they can of items recently taught.
Focus	The written and spoken form and meaning of single items
Age	Any
Level	Any
Time	Five minutes

Procedure

1 Make sure the board is clean and that students have their books closed, and only a clean sheet of (rough) paper before them.
2 Ask students to write down as many as they can remember of the items learnt for the first time earlier in this lesson, or in the previous lesson.
3 After two or three minutes, write up on the board and say all the items you expected them to remember and allow students to check their lists; add the ones they forgot and correct spelling.
4 Invite them to ask you if there are any items on the board whose meaning they don't remember, and remind them.

Note
This can serve as the introduction to any of the activities based on a 'scatter' of words on the board (see, for example, 2.1.9 *Quick bingo*).

2.1.2 Recall and share

Outline	Students try to recall a set of words after they have been hidden or deleted from the board.
Focus	The spelling (and meaning) of single items
Age	Any
Level	Any
Time	Ten minutes

Procedure

1 Write up on the board in a 'scatter' about ten or twelve words that you want to review. Check they are all understood. Don't let students write them down.

2 Tell the students they have half a minute to 'photograph' the words in their minds, that you are going erase them and they will need to write down as many as they can remember. Tell them how many there are.

3 Delete or hide the words after half a minute, and challenge students to write them down, each working individually.

4 When you see they have stopped writing, tell them to join up in twos or threes (or more) and see if they can together manage to remember them all. They can help each other get the spelling right.

5 Finally, write up again or re-display the original words.

6 Congratulate all those who got them all. The ones who didn't should now copy down the ones they missed. Check that everyone understands the meaning of all items.

Note

If you have projection facilities, or an interactive whiteboard, it's very easy just to switch off the screen display (*Control B*, if you're using PowerPoint®) and then switch it on again, rather than deleting and then rewriting.

 Teaching tip

A lot of useful activities that review lexical items start off with, and are based on, a set of items written up on the board. You will notice that often these are to be written in a 'scatter'– spread randomly round the board, without numbers – rather than in linear or numbered lists. This is because when students are faced with lists laid out in lines they intuitively begin with the first and work down. If you want them to engage with all of the items equally, and in random order, it's best to 'scatter' them.

2.1.3 Words without vowels

Outline	Students reconstruct words they've learnt from words written only with consonants.
Focus	The spelling (and meaning) of recently learnt words
Age	Any
Level	Any
Time	Five–ten minutes

Procedure

1 Write up on the board a set of words you want to review, without their vowels; for example:

    s_st_r f_m_ly for sister, family.

2 Students write down what the full word should be.

3 Invite students to come to the board, two or three at a time, to fill in the missing vowels.

4 Check that all the meanings are understood.

Variations

1 Write up a whole sentence contextualizing the word (the word itself written without vowels).

2 More difficult: write the words without vowels, but without leaving any obvious gaps; for example:

    sstr   fmly.

Note

Students are unlikely to be able to fill in the vowels unless they know the word, including its meaning. So the filling-in is likely in most cases to function also as a review of meaning, reinforced by step 4 of the *Procedure* above.

2.1.4 Single-word dictation

Outline	Students write down from dictation words they have learnt, and check answers.
Focus	The spelling and pronunciation of single items
Age	Any
Level	Any
Time	Five minutes

Procedure

1　Dictate a set of ten or so recently learnt words for students to write down. Make sure these are ones you've reviewed recently and that students are likely to get right.
2　Write up the correct words on the board for students to self-check.
3　Check all the meanings are understood.
4　Ask how well they did: congratulate those who got all or most of them right.

Variations

1　To make dictation easier, provide students with the first letter of each word; or with consonants only (as in the previous activity) so they only have to fill in vowels, or with vowels so they only have to fill in the consonants.
2　To make it more difficult, choose items to dictate which consist of a multi-word expression rather than a single word: you may provide stundents with one of the components in advance, so they just have to fill in the others.

Notes

1　The fact that you are making sure in advance that the students are likely to do this successfully and that you provide immediate feedback and reinforcement make this into a review activity rather than a test. See *4.1.5 Dictation-based tests* for the 'test' version of this.
2　For variations on the basic dictation technique, see *2.1.5 Translation dictation* and *2.2.7 Gapfill dictations* here. See also Morgan, J., & Rinvolucri, M. (1988) *Dictation: New methods, new possibilities.* Cambridge: Cambridge University Press.

○ Teaching tip

I've found that simply reviewing the form (spelling or pronunciation) of items, without overtly focusing on meaning, does, for some reason, also help students to remember meanings. But of course it's always good to add a quick reminder, or elicitation, of meanings after, or during, the spelling check!

2.1.5 Translation dictation

Outline	Students write down the L1 translation of single items dictated by the teacher. This activity is appropriate for classes whose members share the same mother tongue, which is known to the teacher.
Focus	The pronunciation and meaning of items
Age	Pre-adolescent–Adult
Level	Beginner–Intermediate
Time	Five–ten minutes

Procedure

1 Dictate about ten English words or expressions you want to review that have fairly clear-cut L1 equivalents.
2 Students write down only the translation in their L1.
3 Check and write up the translations on the board.
4 Finally, go through the translations you have on the board, and get students to say what the original English word was for each.

Variations

1 Ask students to write down the original English word as well as the translation each time, then check spelling.
2 You can of course do this the other way round: give the L1 equivalents and get students to write down the English. This is a more challenging variation, demanding productive written knowledge of the items.
3 With higher-level classes you might, where there are alternative translations, discuss these and use the discussion to deepen students' awareness of the range, or limitations, of the meanings of the target item.

2.1.6 Guessing

Outline	Students guess items that have been recently learnt.
Focus	The meanings of single items
Age	Young–Adolescent
Level	Any
Time	Ten minutes

Procedure

1 Tell each student to look through the words and expressions they have learnt over the last few weeks (using the coursebook or their own notebooks), and choose one.

2 One student comes to the front of the class.

3 The other students try to guess the item chosen by that student. They ask 'yes/no' questions in order to clarify what sort of a thing it is, and finally (hopefully!) guess it.

4 They are allowed only three 'direct' questions (*Is it a bottle?*). If they don't guess rightly after three direct questions, the student whose word it was has 'won'.

♀ Teaching tip

When doing a guessing activity, make sure that one student isn't doing all the work. If all the class knows the answer and one student doesn't, it's not a good idea to make the guesser ask a number of *yes/no* questions, so that all the rest of class has to do is say *yes* or *no*: far too much work for the guesser, too little for the rest. It needs to be the other way round: if the guessing is based on questioning, then one student needs to know the answer and the rest ask questions. If on the other hand the guessing is based on the provision of hints, as in 2.2.6 *Cuckoo* or 2.1.8 *Guess them fast!*, then the majority of the class need to be hinting and only one or two students guessing.

2.1.7 Draw a word

Outline	Students express the meanings of words in drawings.
Focus	The meanings of single items
Age	Young–Adolescent
Level	Any
Time	15–20 minutes

Procedure

1 Tell students to leaf through their notebooks or coursebooks and each choose one item that the class has recently learnt.
2 Tell students to think about how they might represent their item in a drawing. If the word or expression is abstract, or not something with a clear, tangible representation in the real world, then the drawing will have to be something which represents the student's perception of the concept. For example, a circle might represent *perfection*, a wavering line might represent *uncertain*, an exclamation mark might represent *surprise*.
3 Start off yourself by drawing a word you've chosen. Challenge the class to guess what it is. If they can't guess after a minute or so, tell them what it is and why the drawing represents it.
4 Students take turns drawing their item, eliciting guesses and explaining if necessary.
5 If it's a big class, don't try to get through all the students' drawings in one lesson. This can become tedious: save some for following lessons.

Variation

The same can be done with mime: this is particularly suitable for younger classes.

Notes

1 It's quite possible, of course, that two students will choose the same word. But if it isn't an obvious concrete object they are unlikely to draw it the same way.
2 The discussion of a drawing and its relationship to the target item is likely to raise awareness of aspects of the item's meaning and connotation.

2.1.8 Guess them fast!

Outline	Students get other students to guess words by providing hints.
Focus	The meanings of single items
Age	Any
Level	Any
Time	20 minutes
Preparation	Sets of words, whose members all belong to the same category, to be guessed; you can use the ones shown in *Boxes 2.1.8a, b,* and *c* or ones you prepare yourself that include items you want to review

Procedure

1 Ask one student to come to the front of the class and face the class with their back to the board.

2 Write up five words on the board:

   a mango a banana an apple a lemon a pineapple

3 Tell the rest of the class they have one minute to get the student to guess all five items. They can say what the general category is (*fruit* in this case), and may give any hints they like, but only based on meanings (they may not say *it begins with B*, for example). They may start only when you say *Go.* The student may not ask questions.

4 Say *Go.* Time them, and stop them after a minute even if the student has not guessed everything.

5 If you're not sure they've got the idea, do this again, with another student and a different set of fruits:

   a pear a plum grapes an orange a coconut

6 Divide the class into two teams. The first team sends a representative to stand with their back to the board. You write up a set of items, and the team tries to get their representative to guess what they are within the set time. Then the process is repeated with the other team, using the next set of items (see *Boxes 2.1.8a, b,* and *c* for some suggestions for sets of items at different levels). Meanwhile, you make sure they keep to the allotted time limit, and write up the scores: the current team scores a point for every word successfully guessed in the time.

Variations

1 You may prefer to prepare ready-made sheets of paper with the names of the items to be guessed, so that you can just stick them on the board each time instead of writing them up. Or have them ready on a PowerPoint® presentation or on an interactive whiteboard if you have the necessary equipment.

2 It's quite fun to limit the way the sets of items can be defined: for younger classes guessing animals, for example, you might tell them they can only make their noises (see *1.2.16 Woof! Woof!*) . Some ideas for such limitations applied to different lists are shown in *Box 2.1.8.*

○ Teaching tip

The added 'time limit' component is an important one: it makes for challenge and fun and can often transform even a routine academic exercise into a game-like and enjoyable activity. It also speeds up the interaction, so you get through a lot more material in the time.

Box 2.1.8a: Guess them fast!

Beginner

1. Colours (what things are this colour?)		2. Animals (what are its habits?)	
Team 1	**Team 2**	**Team 1**	**Team 2**
green	red	cat	dog
yellow	blue	mouse	horse
black	white	snake	elephant
brown	orange	lion	bear
grey	purple	giraffe	zebra

3. Actions (mime)		4. Adjectives (mime)	
Team 1	**Team 2**	**Team 1**	**Team 2**
walk	run	big	happy
drink	eat	short	old
look	listen	young	tired
speak	write	fat	long
read	think	angry	quiet

5. People (what do they do?)		6. Things (what do we do with them?)	
Team 1	**Team 2**	**Team 1**	**Team 2**
teacher	singer	pencil	bottle
nurse	mother	clock	glasses
driver	doctor	table	paper
father	student	chair	book
baby	teenager	box	house

Box 2.1.8b: Guess them fast!

Intermediate

1. Professions (what kinds of things do they do?)		2. Places (what do people do there?)	
Team 1	**Team 2**	**Team 1**	**Team 2**
soldier	gardener	hospital	market
chemist	detective	factory	beach
social worker	pilot	petrol station	bus stop
journalist	actor	shopping mall	kitchen
firefighter	secretary	university	bank

3. Feelings (why/when might you feel this?)		4. Homes (who might live there?)	
Team 1	**Team 2**	**Team 1**	**Team 2**
disappointment	hope	castle	cave
fear	relief	caravan	the sea
joy	pity	tent	ship
anger	regret	hole in the ground	hotel
jealousy	excitement	nest	children's home

5. Subjects of study (what might you learn?)		6. Equipment (what would you use it for?)	
Team 1	**Team 2**	**Team 1**	**Team 2**
philosophy	chemistry	laptop	telescope
geography	literature	cellphone/ mobile phone	bicycle
mathematics	engineering	headset	skewer
history	zoology	flashlight/torch	crutches
botany	art	GPS/satnav	satellite dish

Box 2.1.8c: Guess them fast!

Advanced

1. Tools (what do we do with these?)		2. Belief systems (what do they believe?)	
Team 1	**Team 2**	**Team 1**	**Team 2**
screwdriver	hoe	socialism	idealism
hammer	sword	democracy	relativism
scalpel	lasso	fascism	anarchism
needle	nailfile	atheism	despotism
ladle	forceps	post-modernism	agnosticism

3. Company departments/ functions (what do they do?)		4. Verbs (what do they mean?)	
Team 1	**Team 2**	**Team 1**	**Team 2**
personnel	accounts	demonstrate	investigate
marketing	investment	broadcast	implement
research and development	board of directors	neutralize	optimize
		specify	monitor
production	reception	enforce	facilitate
security	IT		

5. Nouns (what do they mean?)		6. Research article terminology (what do they mean?)	
Team 1	**Team 2**	**Team 1**	**Team 2**
perspective	element	methodology	abstract
equivalent	tradition	acknowledge-ments	mean (average)
authority	strategy		
role	migration	correlation	citation
structure	technology	conclusions	footnote
		probability	appendix

2.1.9 Quick bingo

Outline	Students play bingo with new words.
Focus	The spelling, pronunciation and meaning of single words
Age	Young–Adolescent
Level	Any
Time	10–15 minutes

Procedure

1 Write on the board 15 or 20 words you want to review, in a 'scatter'.
2 Tell students to copy down in their notebooks any four of these items.
3 Call out the translation, or definition, of each word in turn, in random order.
4 Any student who has this word crosses it off.
5 The first student to cross off all four words calls out *Bingo* and is the first winner.
6 Continue until all the items have been crossed off. The students who cross off the last word, i.e. the last to finish, are the second winners.

Variations

1 This can be repeated two or three times with the same set of words without students getting bored. But tell students that in the next 'round' they have to copy down different words, not the ones they used previously.
2 A simpler alternative is simply to call out the words themselves, not the definitions or translations. This does not so clearly focus on meaning; but it's quicker, and does provide useful review, with focus on pronunciation, so worth doing it this way if you're in a hurry.
3 Students can be asked to copy out all the words in a square grid divided into three rows of three or four rows of four (so you'd need nine or sixteen words exactly); then the first winner is the one to cross out all the words in a row or column. This version is rather more time consuming, but ensures that all the students write all the words.

Note

The point about having 'first' and 'last' winners is to ensure that you do in fact review all the words on the board, not just the ones up to the point where the first winner finishes, as in a conventional Bingo process. It also allows more winners, and lets students keep hoping they'll win even after the first has finished!

2.1.10 **Remembering pairs**

Outline	Students review single items by playing a memory game (Pelmanism).
Focus	The pronunciation, recognition of written form, and meaning of single items
Age	Young–Pre-adolescent
Level	Beginner (or Intermediate, *Variation 2*)
Time	15–20 minutes
Preparation	A set of pairs of cards. In each pair, one shows a picture and the other the corresponding written word. *Use Boxes 2.1.10a* and *b*, copied and cut out, or make your own. You'll need a set of 30 cards for each small group playing the game.

Procedure

1   Divide the class into groups of three or four students sitting round a table and give each a set of cards.
2   Tell students how to play the memory game:
   • Students put all the cards face down on the table.
   • The first player picks up any two cards, and says out loud what each represents. Other players help if necessary. If the two cards match, the first player keeps them and gets another turn. If not, they return them to the same places, face down.
   • The next player picks up a card; if it corresponds to one already picked up, they try to remember where it was in order to get a matching pair. If not, then they pick up any other card.
3   Students continue to play the game, with each player trying to accumulate as many pairs as possible.

Variations

1   To make the process slightly easier, have the pictures on different-coloured cards from the written definitions, so that the players know they have to pick up one of each colour in order to find a pair.
2   Use the same procedure to practise other kinds of pairs: opposites, synonyms, paired expressions (for example, *to and fro*), compound words (for example, *bookcase*), collocations (for example, *to shake hands*), derivatives (for example, *sense, sensible*).

Box 2.1.10a: Remembering pairs

From *Vocabulary Activities* © Cambridge University Press 2012   PHOTOCOPIABLE

Box 2.1.10b: Remembering pairs

a car	a book	a door	water
a bed	a chair	a table	a pen
a pencil	a window	a boy	a girl
a man	a woman	a foot	a hand
fruit	a baby	a wall	a box

From *Vocabulary Activities* © Cambridge University Press 2012   PHOTOCOPIABLE

2.1.11 Word dominoes

Outline	Students play dominoes using sets of associated words instead of numbers.
Focus	The pronunciation and meanings of sets of nouns
Age	Young–Pre-adolescent
Level	Beginner
Time	20 minutes
Preparation	Sets of dominoes, one set for each small group of students; use *Box 2.1.11*, copied and cut up, or make your own, if you'd like to practise a different set of words.

Procedure

1 Tell students that they are going to play dominoes, but in this case the dominoes are rather different from the usual numbers-based ones. Write up on the board the six topics of the dominoes:

animals clothes people things parts of the body food

2 Explain that while they are playing they may put any animal next to any animal, any thing next to any thing, etc. The rule is, however, that they MUST say both the topic (for example, *things*) and the name of the item (*chair*) before laying down their domino next to a previous *things* domino.

3 Distribute one or two dominoes to each student, stick one up on the board, and invite any student to suggest putting their domino next to it, according to the rules you have explained.

4 After there is a row of ten or so dominoes on the board and you see students have got the idea (you don't have to finish a 'game' at this point), put them into groups and let them play on their own, according to standard domino rules. Each student tries to get rid of all their dominoes, but has to pick one up from a central pile if they can't lay one down when it is their turn. They can, of course, ask each other, or you, to help if they've forgotten the word for something.

♀ Teaching tip

For activities based on pictures, use the coloured version provided on the CD-ROM, if you have a colour printer. If you don't, then colour the pictures yourself or perhaps get the students to do so before laminating and using the pictures in class.

Box 2.1.11: Word dominoes

Continued

Box 2.1.11: Word dominoes (*continued*)

2.1.12 Sort them out (1)

Outline	Students sort items into simple categories.
Focus	The meanings and written forms (receptive) of a mixed set of single words
Age	Young–Adolescent
Level	Beginner–Intermediate
Time	10–15 minutes
Preparation	A mixed list of items the students have learnt belonging to several different categories such as colours, animals, clothing, parts of the body and so on, with a table below to fill in appropriately, copied for students; use *Box 2.1.12* or make your own list.

Procedure

1 Give the students the list of items, laid out as in *Box 2.1.12*, and explain that each fits under one of the headings given.
2 Tell them to copy at least three of the items under each heading; more if they can.
3 If there are students who finish copying all the items into the table while others are still working, invite them to think of more items that are not in the list that they might add to any of the categories given.

Variations

1 To make it easier, provide fewer categories or fewer items: you could, for example, have only two categories: *things* and *people/animals*.
2 You may also give them a set of foods or animals or school subjects and ask them to categorize under *I like it* or *I don't like it*, and then discuss their opinions later.
3 If the students know the concrete items but not the more abstract headings (they might, for example, know *chair, table* but not *furniture*) then provide an L1 translation for these headings.
4 To make it more difficult, provide more items or more difficult categories, such as *feelings, tools, buildings*.
5 Add a few items which don't fit into any of the given categories, and a column headed *Other*: this allows you to include other words you've taught that don't neatly fit into any of the categories.

Box 2.1.12: Sort them out (1)

• a baby	• a book	• an elephant	• kids	• pink	• a table
• a bag	• boots	• a frog	• a man	• red	• a teenager
• a banana	• a clock	• green	• meat	• rice	• a T-shirt
• a bed	• a dog	• a hat	• a mother	• a sheep	• white
• black	• a dress	• jeans	• a pen	• sugar	

Animals	Colours	Things	Food	Clothes	People

From *Vocabulary Activities* © Cambridge University Press 2012   PHOTOCOPIABLE

○ Teaching tip

When giving homework or individual work in class, you can easily provide
different levels of challenge based on the same task. If you say 'Find at least
three items but if you can, then find more,' you fix a criterion for success
that enables slower or less advanced learners to succeed, while retaining
appropriate challenge for the faster or more advanced ones. The key phrase
in the instruction is 'at least': you can apply a similar instruction to most
standard coursebook exercises, thus transforming them into 'differentiated'
tasks.

2.1.13 Sort them out (2)

Outline	Students sort items into different categories: a more complex and demanding version of the previous activity.
Focus	The meanings and written forms (receptive) of sets of items
Age	Adolescent–Adult
Level	Any
Time	10–15 minutes

Procedure

1 Write up on the board items you want to review; make sure students remember all their meanings.

2 Put students into pairs, and challenge them to copy down the items in different columns according to clear criteria they decide on. For example, they might use *parts of speech*; or topics (for example, *the home, people, work, feelings*); or subjective evaluations like *positive* and *negative* or *interesting* and *boring*.

3 Note that they are only allowed to choose categories that have to do with meaning; they can't categorize them by numbers of letters in the word, for example.

4 Teach the word *miscellaneous* if they didn't know it, and tell them that a *miscellaneous* column is allowed for anything that didn't fit into their chosen categories. They are also allowed a *medium/not sure* column if the categories are a pair of opposites, like *positive* and *negative*.

5 When they have finished, share some of the different types of categorization groups have chosen, and if time any explore any uncertainties or disagreements about the categorizations of particular items. This is likely to involve some useful discussion of exact meanings or multiple meanings of items.

Variations

1 You might want to tell students in advance which will be the criteria for classifying, as in the previous activity, rather than letting them decide on their own. Even so, there may be disagreements on where to put a particular item!

2 This activity is simpler to do if the items are all one kind of thing: materials (*glass, iron, wood, gold* . . .) or activities (*sleeping, swimming* . . .), etc. Then you can find clear criteria which relate to these areas, for example: *cheap/expensive* for materials, or *energetic/restful* for activities.

2.1.14 Arrange along a continuum

Outline	Students lay out items in order of priority according to a set criterion.
Focus	The precise meanings and written forms (receptive) of items
Age	Adolescent–Adult
Level	Intermediate–Advanced
Preparation	Sets of six or seven related items, cut up into separate slips of paper, mixed, and put into envelopes, on which is written the suggested criterion; make five or six different sets, four copies (i.e. envelopes) of each. Make two or three copies of a 'key' showing all the correct answers. Use *Boxes 2.1.14a* or *b*, or make up your own.
Time	15–20 minutes

Procedure

1 Write on the board the words:

small big tiny colossal medium smallish huge

Ask students how they would arrange these in order of size. Through discussion, arrive at the order:

tiny small smallish medium big huge colossal

2 Explain the activity to the students:
- Tell the students that they will be working in pairs.
- Each pair will get one envelope with slips of paper showing sets of items like the ones the class has just been working on.
- Students need to arrange these according to the criterion written on the outside of the envelope.
- When they finish, they should check their own answers using the 'key' which should be on your desk, easily available to students as needed.
- Then they should mix the slips again, replace them in the envelope, and take another.

3 Put the students into pairs, and let them start work.

4 Go round helping with any items whose meaning is not clear.

Notes

1 In some cases the order may not be completely clear: for example, it is arguable that *hazardous* and *risky* indicate the same level of danger. Be ready to allow for alternative answers.

2 You may discuss connotation with advanced classes: for example, the word *dated* has a negative connotation, as compared to the positive connotation of *mature*.

Box 2.1.14a: Arrange along a continuum

Intermediate

Criterion: How happy?	Criterion: How loving?	Criterion: How intelligent?	Criterion: How old?	Criterion: How fast?	Criterion: How quietly?	Criterion: How energetic?
sad	hate	idiotic	baby	crawl	scream	sleeping
satisfied	dislike	stupid	child	stroll	shout	watching TV
content	like	silly	teenager	walk	speak loudly	reading
glad	be fond of	average	young adult	march	say	playing chess
happy	love	clever	middle-aged	run	mutter	going shopping
delighted	adore	wise	old	sprint	murmur	hiking
ecstatic	worship	brilliant	ancient	zoom	whisper	working out

Box 2.1.14b: Arrange along a continuum

Advanced

Criterion: How hard?	Criterion: How poor?	Criterion: How dangerous?	Criterion: How old?	Criterion: How enthusiastic?	Criterion: How angry?
diamond	underprivileged	chancy	mature	keen	irritated
steel	reduced	unsafe	dated	eager	upset
glass	impoverished	hazardous	old	excited	annoyed
wood	needy	risky	archaic	inspired	angry
chalk	penniless	dangerous	ancient	enthusiastic	irate
butter	poverty-stricken	perilous	prehistoric	devoted	furious
cotton wool	starving	death-defying	antediluvian	passionate	raging

From *Vocabulary Activities* © Cambridge University Press 2012

2.1.15 Flexible odd one out

Outline	Students identify the odd one out, which may be any one of the given set of words.
Focus	The meanings and written forms (receptive) of sets of words
Age	Pre-adolescent–Adult
Level	Beginner–Intermediate
Time	10–15 minutes
Preparation	Four or five sets of three words that are all the same part of speech and that are in some way 'the same kind of thing'; you might use a selection of words from *Box 2.1.8*, but it's best to make up your own, including in each set at least one word you've taught recently and want to review

Procedure

1 Write up on the board three or four words that are all the same part of speech and that are connected to the same topic. Include in each set at least one word that you want to review; add another two that are associated. For example, if you want to review the word *composer* you might add the associated words *music, piano, song*.

2 Ask students to say which they think is the odd one out. They might suggest that *composer* is the only one which is a person, *piano* is the only instrument, *music* is the only one which is a subject you can learn at school, and *song is* the only one which always involves both words and music.

3 Tick off each item the class has managed to identify as the odd one out. Can they manage to tick them all off?

4 Continue with three or four further similar sets of words.

Variations

1 Use larger sets of words for more challenge; but not more than six.

2 For less advanced classes, allow them to express the reasons for the *odd one out* in L1: the argument may well demand much more advanced language than the items themselves. Even this way, the exercise still demands engagement with the meanings of the target items in English, which is the main aim.

♀ Teaching tip

Tasks such as sorting, prioritizing and finding exceptions involve higher levels of thinking than standard gapfills or matching exercises. They also demand a higher level of engagement with the meanings of the items and therefore arguably learning – as well as being a lot more interesting.

2.1.16 Diamante poems

Outline	Students write a *diamante* poem, using vocabulary they have learnt.
Focus	The meanings and spelling of pairs of antonyms, and other words associated with them
Age	Pre-adolescent–Adult
Level	Intermediate–Advanced
Time	15–30 minutes
Preparation	Thesauri or dictionaries of synonyms and antonyms (paper or digital)

Procedure

1 Ask students to suggest two antonyms; for example: *black* and *white.*
2 Write the first antonym at the top of the board, and the second at the bottom.
3 Then ask them for adjectives: two associated with the first antonym, and two associated with the second: write these in below and above the original words thus:

> black
> dark, scary
>
>
> light, happy
> white

4 Next, ask for verbs associated with the two antonyms, and write them in as *-ing* participles. For example:

> black
> dark, scary
> hiding, shading, closing
>
> shining, brightening, glittering
> light, happy
> white

5 Finally, ask for two nouns, each associated with one of the antonyms, and write them in on a single line in the middle. For example:

black

dark, scary

hiding, shading, closing

witches, night, sunlight, lilies

shining, brightening, glittering

light, happy

white

6 Show students how the whole poem looks like a diamond, and moves from one extreme to the other.

7 Leave the poem on the board as a model. Ask students, individually or in pairs, to think of two antonyms, write them at the top and bottom of a sheet of paper, and create their own diamante poems. They may use thesauri or dictionaries of synonyms and antonyms to help them find words to insert.

8 Students who finish early help those who are still working.

9 Invite students to read out their poems to the class.

Variations

1 Students may write out neatly and decorate their poems, which may then be posted on the classroom wall.

2 More ideas for writing poems based on vocabulary can be found in *Writing Simple Poems*; see acknowledgement below.

Acknowledgement

Adapted from the book *Writing Simple Poems* by Vicki Holmes and Margaret Moulton (see *References and further reading*).

 Teaching tip

Any exercise, such as 2.1.16 *Diamante poems*, that results in aesthetically pleasing results can later be displayed on the wall: not only does this decorate the classroom, it also reminds the students of the vocabulary used. But remember to change the displays regularly: students gradually get used to and stop paying attention to items displayed for more than a couple of weeks, and their impact is lost.

2.2 ITEMS IN CONTEXT

These activities provide opportunities for reviewing vocabulary items as they co-occur with other items in phrases, sentences or longer texts. They also explore distinctions of meaning between different items when compared to one another in meaning-linked sets. They thus help to deepen the learners' knowledge of the way they are used within different contexts and for different purposes.

2.2.1 Search a page

Outline	Students locate the target items in a page of text.
Focus	Reading comprehension of items in context
Age	Adolescent–Adult
Level	Beginner–Intermediate
Time	Five–ten minutes

Procedure

1 Tell students to look at a reading text they have recently been working on and from which you have taught some new vocabulary items.
2 Call out one of the items and challenge students to find it in the text. Students raise their hands as they find it, and underline the sentence or phrase in which it occurs in the text.
3 When you see more than half the students have raised their hands, go on to the next item. Reassure the students that it doesn't matter if not all of them find all the items at this stage; you'll show them all of them later.
4 When you have been through seven to ten items, stop.
5 Call out each item again, but this time a student who found it says where it is (easier if your text provides line numbers!), and reads out the immediate context: the sentence or phrase within which the item appears. Students who didn't find it before can now underline it: help them where necessary.

Variation
Students take turns locating and calling out an item instead of you doing so. In this case you too have to search for and underline it!

2.2.2 Association dominoes

Outline	Students review basic lexical items (nouns) by finding associations between them.
Focus	Meaning and pronunciation of nouns in simple sentence contexts
Age	Young–Pre-adolescent
Level	Beginner–Intermediate
Time	15–20 minutes
Preparation	Cards showing pictures of a range of basic nouns; use *Box 2.2.2* copied for students and cut out, or make a set of your own cards using, for example, drawings from a picture dictionary or from Google Images™. If you have a class of more than 20, make a double set; and you may need to enlarge the pictures if you are working with a large class or in a large room.

Procedure

1 Give two pictures to each student, leaving a pile of reserve pictures on your desk.
2 Stick one picture up in the middle of the board.
3 Tell the students that:
   - Anyone can volunteer to have their card placed beside the one on the board, provided they can think of a good reason why there is an association between the two: for example, they might put a table beside a dog because they both have four legs. The rule is, however, that the same association may not be used twice: so a student may not now add a cat on the basis that it has four legs like a dog! They may, however, add a cat, arguing that both cat and dog are animals.
   - The aim is to make a line that stretches from one side of the board to the other (or draw lines to show 'borders', if the board is too wide!). It is NOT to get rid of dominoes, as in a conventional domino game.
   - Cards may not be added above or below the cards shown; only at the left and right ends of the line.
4 Students continue to volunteer pictures and ideas for associations: put them up as they come.
5 A student who runs out of pictures takes a new one from the pile on your desk.

Variation

Put students into groups and allow them to perform the same activity on their own, laying the cards on the table instead of putting them up on the board.

Box 2.2.2: Association dominoes

From *Vocabulary Activities* © Cambridge University Press 2012   PHOTOCOPIABLE

2.2.3 Connect two

Outline	Students make up sentences that include two of the items from a list.
Focus	Written form and pronunciation of a set of items in simple sentence contexts
Age	Pre-adolescent–Adult
Level	Any
Time	Ten minutes

Procedure

1 Write on the board a set of ten to fifteen items you want to review, in a 'scatter' (not vertical lists or horizontal lines). The items can include both words and multi-word expressions.
2 Invite students to volunteer any sentence they like that contextualizes any two of the items.
3 For the sentence that the student gives, draw a line on the board that connects the two items.
4 Continue until every item has been connected to at least one other.

Variations

1 You'll find that some students soon start creating sentences that link three or more items: that's fine.
2 Other variations that demand sentence contextualization of target items are:
   • Make up sentences that are clearly true.
   • Make up sentences that are clearly false.
   • Make up negative sentences (i.e. that include *not, never* etc.).
   • Make up personalized sentences beginning with *I*.

Follow-up

Point to a line, and ask students to recall what the sentence was that it represents. Delete that line. Carry on until all the lines have been deleted.

 Teaching tip

Just making up sentences to contextualize a particular vocabulary item is pretty boring; it becomes much more interesting if there is some particular challenge, as in the basic task of this activity and the suggestions listed under *Variations*.

2.2.4 About me

Outline	Students use vocabulary they have learnt to write about themselves.
Focus	Spelling, meaning and use of items in sentence contexts
Age	Adolescent–Adult
Level	Intermediate–Advanced
Time	10–15 minutes
Preparation	A list of 20–30 words or *chunks* (multi-word expressions) that have been recently taught or encountered in a recently read text, copied for students or displayed on the board

Procedure

1 Tell students they are going to write sentences which use a selection of these items, but they must be sentences that relate to themselves in some way, and are true.

2 Provide some examples of sentences about yourself that fulfil these conditions, using some of the items on the board.

3 Give students ten minutes to write as many sentences as they can: this has to be done individually. Ask them to write only things they would be willing later to share with the rest of the class – nothing too personal.

4 Students give you their lists of sentences, without adding their names.

5 Read out a set of sentences, correcting any mistakes as you go: the class guesses who wrote them.

Variation

Instead of steps 4 and 5, tell students to get into groups and share their sentences. Later, invite each group to read out to the full class some of the more interesting/original/funny sentences (with the consent of the authors, naturally!).

Follow-up

Have the students display their sentences by putting them up on the wall.

 Teaching tip

With personalized activities like this it is important to have students feel comfortable with what they are sharing about themselves, not to press them to write things they may feel are too intimate or revealing. It is very helpful therefore to demonstrate by doing yourself what you are asking them to do, in an initial 'rehearsal' stage (step 2 above).

2.2.5 True or false

Outline	Students contextualize target vocabulary in true or false statements; other students guess which is true and which is false.
Focus	Pronunciation, meaning and use of items in sentence contexts
Age	Pre-adolescent–Adult
Level	Intermediate–Advanced
Time	15–25 minutes

Procedure

1 Write up on the board ten or twelve items that you want to review, in a 'scatter', not a numbered list.
2 Each student chooses any one of the items and writes down two sentences in which he or she relates the item in some way to him- or herself. One sentence must be true and the other false – but not obviously so!
3 Give the class ten minutes to do this for as many of the items as they can.
4 One volunteer student comes to the board, writes their two sentences on the board and reads them out.
5 The other students ask questions in order to clarify which is true and which is false.
6 Once they have guessed, another student comes to the board and the process is repeated.

 Teaching tip

A lot of activities call for each student, or pair of students, to prepare something to present to the rest of the class. In a large class, it is normally not possible for all the students to present their results in a single lesson. Even if you spread out presentations over two or three lessons, you may not have time for everyone. It's always worth warning students before they start work on this sort of task that not everyone will be able to present. Keep a list of who did present, and make sure that next time other students get priority.

2.2.6 Cuckoo

Outline	Students guess a word from sentences where the word *cuckoo* substitutes for the real word.
Focus	Use of items in sentence contexts
Age	Any
Level	Beginner–Intermediate
Time	15–25 minutes

Procedure

1   One student stands with their back to the board.
2   You write up on the board a word which has not been reviewed for a while, and which the student cannot see.
3   The other students say sentences which provide contexts for this word; but they use *cuckoo* instead of the word itself, which could be any part of speech. For example, if these are beginner students and the real word is *sleep*, they might say:
    We usually cuckoo at night.
Or if it is an advanced class and the word is *vivid*, they might say:
    It was a beautiful day: the sky was a cuckoo blue.
4   The students keep saying more and more sentences until the student at the front of the class guesses the word. He or she may ask questions like
    Can I cuckoo?
5   If the student guesses successfully, he or she gets to choose the next candidate to come to the board. If not, then you choose.

Variations

1   Ask two students, rather than one, to be the 'guessers': this is less stressful, particularly for less advanced students who might be embarrassed at their inability to guess, and will be happy to have someone else with them.
2   For a more demanding version of this, focusing on sets of discrete items, see *2.1.8 Guess them fast!*.

Follow-up

Ask the students to recall some of the *cuckoo* sentences that were said, but this time putting in the real word.

2.2.7 Gapfill dictations

Outline	Students fill in gaps in a text based on teacher dictation.
Focus	Spelling, pronunciation and meaning of a set of items
Age	Any
Level	Beginner–Intermediate
Time	Ten minutes
Preparation	A gapped text (a set of phrases or sentences, or a whole paragraph) where the gaps represent words you want to review; it doesn't have to be obvious what the missing word is in each case, though it sometimes may be.

Procedure

1 Give out the texts and tell students that each gap represents one word they have learnt. Allow them a few minutes to try to fill in any of the words they think they can guess. They may work alone or in pairs.

2 Read out the full text, fairly slowly, but not stopping at each word to give them time to write it down. You'll need to warn them about this, to prevent protests, and reassure them that you'll be reading it again!

3 Give them a couple of minutes to go through, filling in or correcting from memory, and helping each other to complete.

4 Read again, as many times as necessary for all students to finish filling in.

5 Check the answers, including spelling.

Variation

An easier variation is to provide the first letter of the missing word in the text; or the last.

 Teaching tip

When doing vocabulary review based on dictation of a full text, it's a good idea to read out the text several times at normal speed instead of the conventional way (very slowly, pausing to give students time to write). You can do so as many times as are necessary to allow students to fill in all the items. This way you actually go through the text more times, thus providing repeated exposure to the items. Another advantage is the added challenge, as students have to write fast and listen carefully.

2.2.8 Easy cloze

Outline	Students fill in gaps in a passage where the target words are part of the given text, and the gaps are easy to guess.
Focus	Meaning and written form in context
Age	Pre-adolescent–Adult
Level	Any
Time	10–15 minutes
Preparation	Compose a passage or set of sentences that contextualizes the words or expressions you want to review. Alternatively, select and copy sentences from the coursebook that contextualize the target items. Leave the target words untouched, but delete occasional grammatical items like *that, I, she, is, some* – about one per line – and make copies for students. See an example in *Box 2.2.8*, with the target words underlined.

Procedure

1 Give out the texts or sentences and tell students to fill in the gaps. Tell them how long they have to do so.

2 Go round helping, and check as you do so that all the target items are in fact understood by everyone.

3 When time is up, read out the completed text, and students check they have the right answers or fill in ones they'd missed (there may, of course, occasionally be more than one possibility).

Box 2.2.8: Easy cloze

The Eden Project in south-west England was <u>designed</u> as [1]............ centre to <u>educate</u> [2]............ <u>public</u> about [3]............ <u>environment</u>. A number [4]............ greenhouses contain <u>plants</u> [5]............ all around [6]............ world. Eden's <u>designers</u> didn't want the greenhouses to be made out [7]............ <u>glass</u> but instead built out [8]............ a new and lighter <u>material</u>. The opening of the Eden Project [9]............ 2001 was a great <u>success</u> and thousands [10]............ <u>visitors</u> now enjoy visiting the centre [11]............ week.

Adapted from Davis, F. and Rimmer, W. (2011). *Active Grammar*, Unit 34. Cambridge: Cambridge University Press.

2.2.9 Finish the sentences

Outline	Students complete sentences whose beginning includes a target lexical item.
Focus	Written form (receptive), meaning and use of a set of lexical items within sentence contexts
Age	Pre-adolescent–Adult
Level	Any
Time	10–15 minutes
Preparation	A set of unfinished sentences, each of which includes an item you want to review, and which could be completed in all sorts of different ways, copied for students or displayed on the board; at least some of the sentences should elicit personal opinions. See examples in *Box 2.2.9*.

Procedure

1 Distribute or display the unfinished sentences.
2 Each student completes the sentences on their own.
3 Students who finish early are asked to find additional possible endings to the same sentences.
4 When everyone, or almost everyone, has finished, tell students to share their sentences with each other in small groups. The groups decide which are the most interesting/original/funny endings.
5 Share some of the more interesting sentence endings in full class.

 Teaching tip

In principle, it is much more interesting and productive to do completion exercises when the answers are not predetermined but are open to different interpretations so that students complete them using their own imagination, personal preferences or logical thinking. The different answers can be shared later, giving added opportunities for meaningful review of the target items.

Box 2.2.9: Sentence completion

1 I am not <u>afraid of</u> . . .

2 Please don't <u>touch</u> . . .

3 There is a lot of <u>competition</u> in . . .

4 You need <u>muscles</u> in order to . . .

5 There is no <u>snow</u> . . .

6 I did it <u>twice</u> because . . .

7 The water was <u>freezing</u>, but . . .

8 You need <u>therapy</u> if you . . .

2.2.10 Find four collocations

Outline	Students review words by exploring their collocations.
Focus	The written form and meaning of collocations
Age	Adolescent–Adult
Level	Intermediate–Advanced
Time	30 minutes
Preparation	Three or four lists, each consisting of five items you want to review, copied for students or displayed on the board; any one list should consist of items belonging to the same part of speech: verbs, nouns, adjectives or adverbs, and have room to write in collocations. Use dictionaries (paper or digital) and *Box 2.2.10* copied and cut up, or make up your own lists.

Procedure

1 Divide students into pairs or small groups, and give out one list.
2 Tell students that for each item on the list they should try to think of and write down four collocations: other words that they know, or think, 'go with' the target item, either before or after it. These can be full lexical items, or grammatical ones such as prepositions. They may use dictionaries if they are stuck.
3 When a group finds all the collocations it can (even if it hasn't reached four for each item), they get a new list.
4 When the first group has finished all the lists you have prepared, share in full class, and add any more from your own list.
5 Some possible examples of collocations for the items in *Box 2.2.10* are shown in *Answers (Box 2.2.10 Find four collocations)*.

Follow-up

If you have computers easily available, you might continue to *1.3.2 What usually goes with this word? (2)* and let students use corpus-based websites to substantiate or supplement their own intuitions: *British National Corpus* http://corpus.byu.edu/bnc, or the *American Corpus of Contemporary English* http://www.americancorpus.org/, or the *Lextutor* links http://www.lextutor,ca/concordances/concord_e.html/.

Notes

1 Make sure that the students try to think up as many collocations as they can on their own before looking at a corpus, as suggested in the *Follow-up* above. The aim of this activity (in contrast to *1.3.2 What*

usually goes with this word? (2)) is to consolidate and deepen knowledge of the target words on your list rather than to acquire new ones.

2   When preparing your own lists, you'll find that there are substantially fewer adverbs in English than nouns, verbs and adjectives, so perhaps skip the adverb list, or make it much shorter.

♀ Teaching tip

When setting a task for students to do which has, in principle, an unlimited number of answers, it helps a lot to fix a clear, limited goal so that they know when they've finished and what they're aiming for. One possibility is a time limit; another is to say (at least) how many responses they have to find for a given cue. I've found that most students find it more challenging and motivating to think up answers up to a certain given number than just to brainstorm as many as they can.

Box 2.2.10: Find four collocations

Verbs	Nouns	Adjectives	Adverbs
1 spread	1 structure	1 financial	1 generally
....	....	....	....
....	....	....	....
....	....	....	....
....	....	....	....
2 develop	2 furniture	2 miserable	2 eventually
....	....	....	....
....	....	....	....
....	....	....	....
....	....	....	....
3 appreciate	3 season	3 likely	3 honestly
....	....	....	....
....	....	....	....
....	....	....	....
....	....	....	....
4 refuse	4 officer	4 industrial	4 clearly
....	....	....	....
....	....	....	....
....	....	....	....
....	....	....	....
5 argue	5 earth	5 relevant	5 partly
....	....	....	....
....	....	....	....
....	....	....	....
....	....	....	....

Answers (Box 2.2.10 Find four collocations)

Verbs	Nouns	Adjectives	Adverbs
1 spread	1 structure	1 financial	1 generally
spread over	social structure	financial problems	generally accepted
spread across	management structure	financial services	generally speaking
spread throughout	class structure	financial support	generally regarded
spread evenly	complex structure	financial benefits	generally agreed
2 develop	2 furniture	2 miserable	2 eventually
develop properly	antique furniture	miserable life	eventually became
develop skills	pieces of furniture	feel miserable	eventually reached
develop ideas	garden furniture	look miserable	eventually managed
develop into	bedroom furniture	thoroughly miserable	eventually arrived
3 appreciate	3 season	3 likely	3 honestly
appreciate an offer	this/next/last season	likely to	quite honestly
fully appreciate	end of the season	very likely	honestly don't know
appreciate the value of	season ticket	seem likely	honestly believe
appreciate it/that	dry season	most likely	say honestly
4 refuse	4 officer	4 industrial	4 clearly
refuse an offer	chief officer	industrial action	quite clearly
refuse to pay	police officer	industrial waste	clearly defined
absolutely refuse	senior officer	industrial development	clearly visible
refuse to allow	medical officer	industrial dispute	clearly shows
5 argue	5 earth	5 relevant	5 partly
argue a case	what/how on earth..?	relevant information	partly because
argue in favour of	surface of the earth	particularly relevant	at least partly
argue about	heaven and earth	relevant factors	wholly or partly
argue with	down to earth	relevant facts	partly responsible

2.2.11 Rewrite more simply

Outline	Students simplify a passage that contextualizes target vocabulary.
Focus	The written form (receptive) and meaning of items in context
Age	Adolescent–Adult
Level	Intermediate–Advanced
Time	25 minutes

Procedure

1 Select a paragraph or so from a text your class has recently been working on and from which you have taught some new vocabulary.

2 Tell your students they have to rewrite this extract in order to make it comprehensible to other students who don't know English as well as they do.

3 Work on the first sentence together, and write up on the board the simplified version the class and you have composed. Note that you will find that you are simplifying the grammar as well, but it's mainly the lexical items for which you'll need to look for easier alternatives.

4 Give students ten minutes to do the same, with the rest of the paragraph, as much as they have time for.

5 Compare results orally (without necessarily writing up the entire simplified text on the board).

Follow-up

Discuss with students what meanings, or implications, have been lost by the simplification.

Note

Your students should be aware that this kind of simplification is a useful communication strategy. They may well find themselves in the future in situations where they need to interact with people who know a lot less English than they do, and therefore need to find simpler alternatives to the more advanced vocabulary they know and could use.

2.2.12 Which did I erase?

Outline	Students identify items erased from a text on the board.
Focus	The written form (receptive) and pronunciation of items in context
Age	Young
Level	Beginner
Time	Five–ten minutes

Procedure

1 Write on the board an extract from a text you have recently studied, including items you want to review.
2 Tell students to close their eyes.
3 Delete one of the target items.
4 Students open their eyes and identify which item is missing.
5 Do the same again, until you have deleted all the items, while the surrounding context remains on the board.
6 Tell students to read aloud the whole text, inserting the missing items as they do so.

Variation
It is, of course, most convenient to do this activity, if you have the facilities, by using a data projector or interactive whiteboard, and use word-processing tools to delete individual words.

2.2.13 Gradual erase

Outline	Students recall a text gradually erased from the board.
Focus	The written form (receptive), pronunciation (and meaning) of items in context
Age	Young–Pre-adolescent
Level	Beginner–Intermediate
Time	Five–ten minutes

Procedure

1 Write on the board an extract of up to about 50 words from a text you have recently studied, including items you want to review.
2 Delete a phrase or two, between three and five words (students don't need to close their eyes as you do so).
3 Students read out the whole text, including the bit that is missing.
4 Continue to delete a few words each time, so that each time students have to 'read' more and more of the text from memory, until the board is empty and they have memorized the entire extract.
5 Students try to write down the whole text from memory: they can work in pairs and help each other.
6 Finally, write up the text again so that students can check themselves, including the spelling of the target vocabulary items.

Note

This looks like a mechanical 'parrotting' activity, but in fact it is difficult to memorize texts in this way unless you understand them; it therefore helps students remember items within their accompanying contexts.

2.2.14 Once upon a time

Outline	Students make up a story that includes all the words or expressions from a list.
Focus	The written form (receptive), pronunciation, meaning and use of items in context
Age	Any
Level	Intermediate–Advanced
Time	10–15 minutes
Preparation	A list of 15–30 words or expressions you want to review (preferably not all from the same text), displayed on the board or copied for students

Procedure

1 Put students into groups of three or four, and tell them to make up a story which has to include all the words you want to review. Start them off with the words: *Once upon a time*... All members of the group should contribute. They do not have to write down the story.
2 A 'secretary' ticks off the words as they use them: the secretary may also, of course, participate in the telling of the story.
3 The activity ends when the first group has managed to integrate all their items into their story.

Variations

1 Give each student a particular subset of the target items; that student has to find a way of weaving their own items into the narrative.
2 Prepare, or ask students to prepare, a set of slips each with one item on it. The slips are placed face down on the table. Students take turns picking up a slip and use the word in their bit of the story.

Follow-up

Say one of the items, and ask the different groups how this item fitted into their stories. Use this follow-up to provide extra review of items you feel are particularly tricky or difficult to remember.

Note

You will find that as the process of storytelling goes on, some groups begin to laugh: the necessity of including sometimes incongruous items in the same context makes for humour.

2.2.15 Dicto-gloss

Outline	Students note down key words from a listening passage and try to reconstruct the original text.
Focus	The pronunciation, spelling, meaning and use of items in context
Age	Adolescent–Adult
Level	Intermediate–Advanced
Time	20–30 minutes
Preparation	The passage you have chosen, available to be shown on the board later in the activity, or copied for students

Procedure

1 Choose or compose a passage which includes items you want to review: it should be not more than ten or twelve lines (about 100–120 words) long.
2 Tell students you are going to read it out to them; they need to take notes in order to reconstruct it later as accurately as they can.
3 Read out the passage twice, at normal speed; students take notes.
4 Students work in groups to try to reconstruct the original passage, in writing. Go round groups and help with any vocabulary they may have forgotten.
5 When they have been working for about ten minutes, read out the passage again.
6 Students continue to work for another ten minutes.
7 Distribute the copies of the passage, or display on the board.
8 Discuss with students what they got right and where they went wrong.

Note

This procedure is also an excellent basis for work on grammar and cohesion.

Acknowledgement

This idea is based on Ruth Wajnryb's book *Grammar Dictation* (see *References and further reading*).

 Teaching tip

When students are working at similar tasks, and you want them all to finish, there is always a problem that some students finish before others. One solution, which has been suggested earlier, is to provide a 'reserve' task for the faster workers to do; another, less conventional but in many ways more educational, is to get the faster workers to help the slower until everyone has finished.

2.2.16 Rhymes and couplets

Outline	Students find rhymes and use them to create poems.
Focus	The pronunciation, meaning and use of items in context
Age	Any
Level	Beginner–Intermediate
Time	30 minutes

Procedure

1   Introduce students to the word *rhyme* in English, and get them to suggest rhymes to a few simple words like: *make, do, late, buy, chair, floor, in, at* . . . .

2   Tell each student to choose a word out of a text that they have recently studied, and think of at least one word that rhymes with it. If they cannot find a word that rhymes, they may ask you to teach them one. (If even you can't find one, they may change the original word!)

3   Once they have a pair of rhymes (say *chair, fair*), they have to compose a poem of two lines (a *couplet*); the lines each end with one of the rhyming words. For example:

    It's not fair
    That my father always gets the best chair.

4   Note that the couplet has to make a grammatical sentence, but does not have to *scan* (have a strict, uniform, rhythm). It just has to rhyme. This sort of poem is sometimes called a *clerihew*. It may often convey a funny, personal, or nonsensical message.

5   Any student who completes their rhyme looks around for another student who has not yet done so, and helps them. The last students to finish may find five or six classmates helping them to do so!

6   The students write out their own couplets neatly, with illustrations or decorations, and post them on the classroom wall for all to enjoy.

Variations

1   You may make the task more challenging by adding conditions. For example, the couplet has to state something that is true; or it has to deal with a topic that you have determined in advance (*animals, the school, the English language, the circus* . . .).

2   Students choose two words, for each of which they have to find a rhyme, and make up a poem of four lines; but it still has to make sense!

3   Students write out their poems for publication using word-processing facilities and the illustrations that are available through computer software or the Internet.

3 Advanced vocabulary study

The activities here are for more advanced or academic classes who will benefit from further use of dictionaries, thesauri and corpora, as well as from exploring subtle distinctions of meaning and form of lexical items and their etymological development.

3.1 USING DICTIONARIES AND THESAURI

These activities help students become more effective users of vocabulary reference books.

3.1.1 What can the dictionary tell me?

Outline	Students compare their dictionaries, and learn what information they can get from them.
Focus	Awareness of the components of dictionary entries; evaluation of different dictionaries
Age	Adolescent–Adult
Level	Intermediate–Advanced
Time	30–40 minutes
Preparation	A set of not more than seven different dictionaries, two or three copies of each; *Box 3.1.1*, copied for students

Procedure

1   Distribute the forms shown in *Box 3.1.1*. Write up the names of the dictionaries on the board, labelling each with a letter (*A*, *B*, *C*, etc.), which students will later refer to when completing the form in *Box 3.1.1*.
2   Make sure all the components of the form are understood.
3   Put students into pairs and give each one a dictionary. Put the remaining dictionaries on a desk or chair at the front of the class.
4   Write on the board five words which the students have recently studied, and tell them to look these up in 'their' dictionary.
5   Using the form provided, students fill in the title of the dictionary in the space provided, and note which of the added bits of information the dictionary includes.
6   When the first group has finished studying all the different dictionaries you have, or when you feel that the group is running out of energy or time, stop them and come together to discuss results.
7   Discuss which dictionary, on the whole, the students thought was best, and why. Consider which you like best, and why. List the advantages/ disadvantages of the different dictionaries.

Box 3.1.1: What can the dictionary tell me?

Does the dictionary give you the following information? Tick (✓) the appropriate column.	A	B	C	D	E	F	G
1 Part of speech (noun, verb, etc.)							
2 Pronunciation							
3 Other forms (plurals of nouns, past tenses of verbs, etc.)							
4 Main meaning, clearly translated or explained							
5 Examples of sentences that use the word in this meaning							
6 Other meanings							
7 Examples of sentences that use the word in these meanings							
8 Other words that the target word often occurs with (collocations)							
9 Particular idiomatic expressions that use the word							
10 Extra information (for example, if it is formal/informal/American or British English, taboo, etc.). If you write ✓, write details below							

Extra information:

A: _____

B: _____

C: _____

D: _____

E: _____

F: _____

G: _____

3.1.2 What can the thesaurus tell me?

Outline	Students look up concepts in the thesaurus to explore its possibilities, and consider how the thesaurus might aid their own language development.
Focus	Using a thesaurus
Age	Adolescent–Adult
Level	Intermediate–Advanced
Time	20–30 minutes
Preparation	For advanced students: *Roget's Thesaurus of English words and phrases*; enough copies for each pair of students to have one (see *References and further reading*); alternatively, online thesaurus: websites (see *Note* below); for intermediate students: dictionaries of synonyms, or websites providing them

Procedure

1 Explain to students what a thesaurus is: a collection of words and phrases grouped according to conceptual fields: *joy*, for example, or *agriculture*. Looking up one word, therefore, will take you to a conceptual field that the word belongs to (there may be several, if the word has more than one meaning), and to all the other words and expressions that also belong there. For example, if you look up *happiness*, the thesaurus will refer you to the area of *joy*, where you will find all sorts of other words that mean similar things, and associated adjectives, adverbs and verbs.

2 Give the class a concept such as *chair*: what sorts of words and phrases do they think will be in the same section of the thesaurus? List on the board all the ideas they have.

3 Now tell them to look up the word in a thesaurus or dictionary of synonyms and see what they can find. (Note that in a thesaurus, *chair* comes under the general concept of *support*; but they can easily find it by looking up *chair* in the index at the end of the book.)

4 Explain as necessary new items that students have found in the thesaurus. (Though in my experience there may be ones we don't know ourselves and have to look up!)

5 Hold an open discussion: in what ways can a thesaurus help students' English? Some possible conclusions are:
   - If I simply want to enlarge my vocabulary in a particular area, I can browse through the relevant section of the thesaurus.
   - If I want to find whole phrases, and not just single-word synonyms, the full thesaurus will provide them.

- If I can remember that there is a word for what I want in English, but can't remember what it is (*It's on the tip of my tongue, but ...*), looking up a synonym in the thesaurus will usually reveal it.
- If I'm writing and don't want to repeat myself, the thesaurus will suggest alternatives.

Note

Most online thesauri, even if they are called 'Roget's Thesaurus' are actually dictionaries of synonyms, providing a useful set of words that mean the same sort of thing as your search word. They lack, however, the rich variety of formulaic expressions, idioms and quotations that can be found in the paper or CD-ROM version of the original *Roget's Thesaurus of English words and phrases* published by Penguin or Oxford University Press. The online version that is the nearest I have found to the real thing is at http://poets.notredame.ac.jp/Roget/. There are also learner dictionaries which provide a rich selection of synonyms and parallel expressions for any word you look up: the *Longman Language Activator*, for example (see *References and further reading*).

3.1.3 Looking up words faster

Outline	Students see how quickly they can find items in a dictionary.
Focus	Increasing speed of locating items in a dictionary
Age	Pre-adolescent–Adult
Level	Any
Time	10–15 minutes
Preparation	Dictionaries: one per student; two lists of twenty words each that you want to teach or review

Procedure

1 Tell students that they're going to do an activity which will increase their speed of looking up items in a dictionary.
2 Distribute the first list of words: tell students not to start looking them up until you say *Go*.
3 Tell them they have four minutes to find as many of the words as they can. They should simply write the page number by each word as they find it.
4 Say *Go*, and then *Stop* after four minutes. Ask students to count up how many they found and note the number.
5 Give out the second list, tell students they're going to do the same again and should try to break their previous record.
6 Repeat step 4 and get students to count up again.

Variations

1 If students all have the same dictionary, then you can prepare the answers in advance (a page number for each word), and check at the end of each 'round' of looking up.
2 Again if students all have the same dictionary this could be run as a competition: the first to find all the items says *Stop*, and (if all their answers are right) is the winner. But see *Teaching tip* below.

Follow-up

Do the same again a few lessons later, and see if students continue improving their looking-up speed.

 Teaching tip

Competing against oneself (trying to break your previous record) is in principle a more motivating strategy than competing against others ('Who can get the best result?'). The problem with conventional competitions is that they are rather demoralizing for the weaker students who very often lose; competing against yourself, everyone can 'win'.

3.1.4 Guess it first

Outline	Students guess the meaning of a word before looking it up in the dictionary.
Focus	Finding the right meaning in a dictionary for a particular context
Age	Any
Level	Intermediate–Advanced
Time	15–30 minutes
Preparation	Dictionaries (paper or digital); a short reading text with some new words in it, copied for students

Procedure

1 Tell students to read through the text and copy onto a separate piece of paper those words or expressions they don't understand.

2 Next to each item they have copied, students write more or less the 'sort of thing' they think the item means (they can do this in L1). For example, if they have a sentence like *The town is located amid gentle pine-covered hills* and they have noted *amid* and *pine*, they could guess that *amid* might mean something like *on* or *near*, and must be a preposition; and *pine* is a noun and must mean some kind of vegetation or stone.

3 Only when students have finished writing their guesses may they go to the dictionary and check out the answers.

4 Verify the answers they have found in full class, and compare these with their guesses.

5 Show them how their guesses narrowed down the possibilities when they were looking up the word, thus speeding up the looking-up process and making it more likely that they would find the right word.

Variation

When students have finished writing their guesses in pairs, tell them to join another pair and see if they can help each other define their guesses more precisely before looking them up.

 Teaching tip

It's worth telling students to use regularly the strategy of thinking in advance about what meaning they think the target word or expression might have, before looking it up. They don't need to write this down, just keep it in mind as they refer to the dictionary.

3.2 EXPLORING VOCABULARY ITEMS

These activities provide students with opportunities to find out more
about the meaning, *morphology, etymology* (source, possibly from
another language) or communicative use of items of vocabulary they have
encountered previously. The aim is to deepen rather than broaden the
students' vocabulary knowledge.

3.2.1 It doesn't mean quite the same thing (1)

Outline	Students pinpoint subtle differences between words that have similar meanings.
Focus	Differences between the meanings of apparent synonyms
Age	Adolescent–Adult
Level	Intermediate–Advanced
Time	30–40 minutes
Preparation	Pairs of (or sets of three) synonyms: use examples from *Box 3.2.1* or, preferably, compile your own. Select a few words you've recently taught in class and look for rough synonyms of them. You may find it useful to refer to a (print or digital) thesaurus or dictionary of synonyms.

Procedure

1 Discuss the concept of synonymity with students. Tell them that:
   - There are few, if any, absolute synonyms within a language (i.e. words that mean exactly the same and are always interchangeable).
   - Normally there are differences between synonyms. These may be distinctions of actual real-world meaning (for example, *table/desk*), of intensity (for example, *small/tiny*), of connotation or negative/ positive associations (for example, *damp* (negative)/*moist* (positive)), of formality (for example, *guy/man*), of collocation (for example, *tall* (tends to go with *people* or *trees*)/*high* (tends to go with *mountain* or abstracts like *level, quality*, etc.), of localized usage (for example, *lift* in British English versus *elevator* in American) or of technical or professional vs general 'lay' terminology (for example, *precipitation/ rain*).
2 Write up on the board five words, each of which has at least one obvious synonym (perhaps choose from the lists in *Box 3.2.1*) and elicit their synonyms from students.

3 Give students five minutes to work in pairs or threes and decide between themselves what distinctions there are between the pairs of synonyms. They can use dictionaries if easily available, or other tools (see *Variations* below). They don't need to write anything down.

4 Elicit their ideas in the full class; correct and add your own ideas if appropriate.

Variations

1 More advanced students can also check out the differences between the synonyms by using concordance tools of a corpus (the *British National Corpus* at http://corpus.byu.edu/bnc/; or the *Corpus of Contemporary American English* at http://www.americancorpus.org/; or a selection of corpora at the *Lextutor* website *Corpus Concordance English* http://www.lextutor.ca/concordancers/concord_e.html). If you have time, prepare in advance lines of concordances of the words you have chosen for students to study in order to work out the differences for themselves.

2 Another useful website for students to use is *Wordnik*: http://www.wordnik.com/. Enter a word in the box provided, click *Thesaurus* and then click on the *Search* icon. The results will give you synonyms, among which the one(s) chosen is/are bound to appear. You can now click on the boxes to the left of the synonyms you want to know about in order to see dictionary definitions which clarify the differences.

Follow-ups

1 For homework, ask students to find other pairs of synonyms they know and could share with the class, together with the subtle distinctions between them.

2 Encourage students to look for and bring to share in class synonyms they come across in their own reading.

Note

There are lots of synonym sites on the Internet (just Google™ the word *synonyms*), but they do not normally provide any help with identifying subtle distinctions between synonyms; for that you need a good dictionary.

Box 3.2.1: It doesn't mean quite the same thing (1)

Intermediate

- apartment/flat
- children/kids
- donate/give
- educate/teach
- lamp/light
- macho/masculine
- orchestra/band
- pal/mate
- policeman/police officer
- seat/chair
- strength/power
- surprised/astonished

Advanced

- attorney/lawyer/solicitor
- enemy/antagonist/foe
- excellent/superb/outstanding
- famous/notorious/well-known
- forge/falsify/counterfeit
- medication/medicine
- offspring/children/issue
- select/choose/elect
- slip/slide/skid
- slim/thin/skinny
- subway/underground
- toil/work/labour

3.2.2 It doesn't mean quite the same thing (2)

Outline	Students who share the same mother tongue explore differences between English words or expressions and parallel items in their L1.
Focus	Differences between the meanings of lexical items in different languages
Age	Adolescent–Adult
Level	Intermediate–Advanced
Time	20 minutes (spread over two lessons)

Procedure

1 Ask students to look at their vocabulary notebooks and read out some items they've written down over the last couple of weeks, together with their L1 equivalents.

2 Write them up on the board quickly, until you have ten to fifteen items.

3 Ask the students: which of these are exact translations, in your opinion? They may find one or two (see *Note* below), but in most cases you will be able to show them that there are differences, either of actual denotational meaning, or of the range of other words it can collocate with.

4 Tell your students to choose six other similar items from their notebooks for homework and to try to define and write down the differences between the English word and an obvious L1 translation. They may use dictionaries or consult informants who know both languages well.

5 Remind students that they should be looking for two main kinds of distinctions:

   a) actual differences in meaning (Is the English word more, or less, specific than the L1 one? Does it refer perhaps to a real-world object or phenomenon that is slightly different in the L1 culture? Does it have slightly different connotations?)

   b) differences of collocation (Which other words can the English word combine with, and does the L1 combine with different ones?).

6 Take in and check their results.

7 In the next lesson, present to the class a selection from the students' work: differences between the translations that you think are particularly useful or interesting.

Note

There do exist some one-to-one precise translations between languages: for example, the item may be a scientific or academic term used internationally; or the L1 word or expression may have been coined (invented) or actually borrowed from English in order to express the meaning of the original English one. But in most cases there will be differences.

♀ Teaching tip

It's important to make students aware of the fact that L1 translations are usually not exact equivalents of the target language item. That said, translations do provide quick and easily understood explanations of meanings, and it's really helpful to use them at first encounter with a new item. You can always go into more detail about the finer distinctions later.

3.2.3 Analysing meanings

Outline	Students analyse sets of words using componential analysis.
Focus	Differences in meaning between sets of words with the same general meaning
Age	Adolescent–Adult
Level	Advanced
Time	30 minutes
Preparation	Dictionaries, (paper or digital); matrices of words as shown in *Box 3.2.3a* and a selection of words for analysis from *Box 3.2.3b*

Procedure

1 Write on the board a simple word that is usually learnt early on in language study: for example, *walk* or *book*.

2 Challenge students to suggest some more advanced words they know that refer basically to the same concept. They might add to *walk* the items *march, hike*; and to *book: paperback, hardback*. When they have exhausted their own knowledge, add a couple more of your own: *stride, stagger, limp; tome, volume*.

3 Analyse the words you have gathered using a componential analysis in a *matrix*, as shown in *Box 3.2.3a*. The plus and minus signs are self-explanatory; *n* means 'neutral'. If you aren't sure, insert a question mark.

4 Give the students another set of similar items (some suggestions may be found in *Box 3.2.3b*), and challenge them to do the same on their own, individually or in pairs. They may use dictionaries.

Notes

1 This is a rather time-consuming exercise, though many students find it interesting. Its main goal is simply to raise awareness of aspects of meaning, which hopefully will help students as they learn new items.

2 A simpler form of this activity, demanding the ordering of items according to a specified criterion, can be found at *2.1.14 Arrange along a continuum*.

Box 3.2.3a: Analysing meanings

	go by foot	a long distance	with purpose	fairly fast	evenly	other associations
walk	+	n	n	n	n	n
march	+	+	+	+	+	military
hike	+	+	+	+	+	leisure-time activity, enjoyment
stride	+	–	++	+	+	dominance, energy
stagger	+	–	–	–	?	drunkenness, or weakness
limp	+	–	–	–	–	one foot/leg not working properly

	serious content	size and weight	durable	formal register	other associations
book	n	n	n	n	n
paperback	–	–	–	–	readable
hardback	n	+	+	–	expensive
booklet	n	– –	–	–	informative
volume	+	+	+	+	academic
tome	++	+++	+	++	ironic

Box 3.2.3b: Analysing meanings

1   false, artificial, counterfeit, synthetic, forged
    Criteria: fabric, coins, documents, negative

2   real, authentic, true, genuine, original
    Criteria: quotation, statement, painting, language

3   chair, stool, throne, bench, armchair, sofa
    Criteria: with a back, with armrests, comfortable, royal, in the park

4   hat, beret, bowler, cap, helmet, bonnet
    Criteria: hard, soft, for a man, for a woman, for a soldier

5   shoes, boots, sandals, slippers, clogs, trainers
    Criteria: in the house, for outdoors, sports, heavy, light

6   criminal, offender, delinquent, thief, crook, villain
    Criteria: legal definition, colloquial insult, probably commits a serious crime

7   fly, float, glide, soar, flutter, hover
    Criteria: fast, on the spot, a bird, a plane, a helicopter, a balloon

8   talk, converse, chat, gossip, lecture, address
    Criteria: formal, informal, academic, usually two or three people,
    with an audience

9   want, desire, wish for, feel like, crave, fancy
    Criteria: mild, extreme, something here and now, something imagined or distant

10 run, sprint, canter, jog, trot
    Criteria: a horse, a person, fast, short distance

11 hurt, harm, wound, injure, damage
    Criteria: a person, a thing, reputation, vanity

12 red, rosy, florid, flushed, crimson
    Criteria: dark colour, light colour, cheeks, blood

13 fat, obese, stout, plump, chubby, overweight
    Criteria: extreme, positive, negative, baby

14 good-looking, lovely, handsome, attractive, pretty
    Criteria: man, woman, picture, view

3.2.4 Translation bloopers

Outline	Students in a monolingual class analyse the inaccuracies in a computer translation.
Focus	Analysis of mismatches between L1 and English translations
Age	Adolescent–Adult
Level	Intermediate–Advanced
Time	15 minutes
Preparation	A short English text at a level of difficulty appropriate for the class together with its computer translation (try using Google™ Translate http://translate.google.com/), displayed on the board or copied for students

Procedure

1 Distribute or display the two texts, and invite students to underline any translations they feel are inaccurate or inappropriate. They can use dictionaries as needed.
2 Discuss these mistranslations in full class: why did they occur?
3 Draw students' attention to the relevant aspects of meaning of the L1 or English vocabulary items that caused the computer program to translate the way it did.

Variation

Do it the other way round: start from an L1 text and look at the English translation.

Follow-ups

1 Tell students for homework to feed in a similar text to their computers and elicit a translation; then analyse it the same way on their own, and bring their findings to the following lesson for discussion.
2 For more advanced students, perhaps discuss: how could computer translations become more accurate? Or will computer translations never be as good as human ones?

 Teaching tip

3.2.4 *Translation bloopers* is a good example of how mistakes can furnish a basis for interesting and useful learning. Point this out to your students, and encourage them to see their own errors in a similarly positive light: as a way to learn rather than evidence of failure.

3.2.5 What's the best way to translate . . . ?

Outline	Students in a monolingual class translate selected items from a text.
Focus	Study of precise meanings of lexical items in context, through translation into L1
Age	Adolescent–Adult
Level	Advanced
Time	20 minutes
Preparation	A text copied for students or taken from the coursebook, where you have noted or underlined between five and ten items – brief phrases or collocations – whose meaning is complex, or whose translation might be problematic; see sample text in *Box 3.2.5*

Procedure

1 If you have not been able to mark the target items on the students' copies of the text, then write up on the board the words or phrases that you want them to translate.
2 Give students a few minutes to write down their chosen translation of each item into L1.
3 Share and compare results, and discuss the problems of meaning which may have come up. Try to come to a consensus about the best translation(s).

Variation

Do the same the other way round: select a text in the students' mother tongue and ask them to translate key phrases into English.

Box 3.2.5: What's the best way to translate ...?

Sample text

The phrase [1]'a born teacher' is not usually meant [2]to be taken literally. People who use it do not [3]seriously mean that someone is born with a certain [4]teaching DNA configuration in their genes. They are, rather, referring to [5]stable personality characteristics, [6]resulting from a combination of [7]innate and environmental influences, that the teacher brings to their [8]professional practice and that produce something that looks like a [9]natural bent for teaching.

3.2.6 Literal or metaphorical?

Outline	Students brainstorm literal and figurative meanings of selected lexical items.
Focus	Exploring the figurative meaning of terms whose meaning was originally simple objects or actions
Age	Adolescent–Adult
Level	Advanced
Time	30–45 minutes
Preparation	A sample concordance page: use *Box 3.2.6a*, copied for students or displayed on the board, or make up your own; a selection of words from *Box 3.2.6b*

Procedure

1 Write the word *head* on the board. Discuss with students the literal and metaphorical meanings of the word. How many metaphorical meanings can they think of? Suggest or elicit expressions like *the head of a company, the head of a school, heads of government, at the head of the procession.*

2 Broaden the question to include contexts where the word is functioning as a different part of speech: *to head a revolution, to head for ...*; or as part of a compound word: *headmaster, headword.*

3 Invite students to look at a corpus concordance page of 50 lines showing the word *head* as it occurs in natural contexts (see *Box 3.2.6a*). What other metaphorical meanings can they find?

4 Provide another word – a noun, verb, or adjective – that refers to something concrete in the real world (see examples in *Box 3.2.6b*, and elicit metaphorical meanings for it that students already know: then send them to a concordancing tool to look for further meanings for themselves (see *Note* below for useful concordance websites). This can be done for homework if online computers are not easily available in class; or see *Variation 1* below.

5 Discuss the students' findings in class: which meanings appear to be most frequent?

Variations

1 If you do not have easy access to the Internet, send your students to search for the information in a dictionary. Good learners' dictionaries usually give information on how frequent the item is, but may not always provide sample contexts for the different meanings.

2   At step 4, divide students into small groups and give each group a
    different word; later, pool their findings in full class.
3   Combine this activity with *1.3.1 What usually goes with this word? (1)*:
    tell students to look not only for new meanings, but also for the most
    common multi-word expressions within which they occur.

Note

Useful websites you can use for this activity are: the *Lextutor* concordancing
site: http://www.lextutor.ca/concordancers/concord_e.html; or the *British National
Corpus*: http://corpus.byu.edu/bnc/; or the *American Corpus of Contemporary
English*: http://www.americancorpus.org/.

⊙ Teaching tip

Even if you intend to use reference books or websites as a basis for an activity,
don't tell students to go straight to them at the beginning of the procedure:
it's always worth eliciting first what the students know between them, and
then use the reference materials to expand, confirm or refine their previous
knowledge.

Box 3.2.6a: Literal or metaphorical?

. . . will wind up its 1961 session Monday and <u>head</u> for home where some of the highway bond . . .
. . . and was able to save place money only a <u>head</u> in front of Glen T. Hallowell's Milties . . .
. . . Philadelphia Eagles, was elevated today to <u>head</u> coach. Skorich received a three-year contract . . .
. . . luncheon in the Teter House. Mrs Roger Mead is <u>head</u> of the luncheon table decorations . . .
. . . kids and comic books in the back seat, and <u>head</u> for home. And where is 'home', that . . .
. . . at Kercheval Monday afternoon when a car <u>heading</u> north on Belvidere stopped belatedly . . .
. . . Dr Hester, also one of the youngest men ever to <u>head</u> a major American university, succeeds . . .
. . . for the 1970s here Tuesday by Peter G. Peterson, <u>head</u> of one of the world's greatest camera firms, . . .
. . . associate curator of education. Miss Bouton <u>headed</u> up one of the four groups that went on . . .
. . . with the two men, 'is that both realize Mantle is <u>head</u> and shoulders above Maris'.) Hitting, Mantle . . .
. . . Washington, this approach might be expected to <u>head</u> off Mr Khrushchev for the moment. But because . . .
. . . the incident is how much longer will UN bury its <u>head</u> in the sand on the Congo problem instead . . .
. . . Katanga. That notion is fantastically wrong-<u>headed</u> from several points of view. The UN army is . . .
. . . 100 million tons of TNT, to knock sense into the <u>heads</u> of those backward oafs who can't see the . . .

From *Vocabulary Activities* © Cambridge University Press 2012   PHOTOCOPIABLE

Box 3.2.6b: Literal or metaphorical?

• light	• arms	• fall	• feel
• sharp	• body	• jump	• hear
• straight	• eye	• lie	• say
• sweet	• face	• run	• taste
• thick	• hand	• stand	• touch
• branch	• broad	• bright	• field
• fertile	• high	• clear	• ground
• plant	• long	• hard	• outlook
• root	• narrow	• low	• peak
• stem	• short	• soft	• way

3.2.7 Related words

Outline	Students extend their awareness of areas of meaning by looking up associated words and phrases in a thesaurus.
Focus	Vocabulary expansion through use of reference books
Age	Adolescent–Adult
Level	Intermediate–Advanced
Time	20 minutes
Preparation	Dictionaries, thesauri; words selected from *Box 3.2.7*, or suggested by students

Procedure

1 Write the word *bag* in the middle of the board.
2 Identify the *superordinate* (the general category to which the main word belongs) – in this case *containers*. Delete *bag* and write *containers*. Start adding further items around the new headings, joined to it by lines; for example:

boxtinsackbottlecupbasket

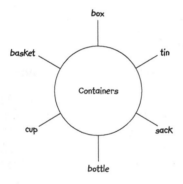

3 Ask students to check their thesauri, and find more words and expressions that could be added. Elicit their findings and add them to the list on the board.
4 Ask students in groups to select another base word of their own choice (or give them suggestions from *Box 3.2.7*), identify the superordinate, and try to find items that belong to it.
5 Each group presents its findings to the class.

Variations

1   Instead of steps 4 and 5, ask students to work on their own for homework, on a word of their choice. They should write up the results as a poster – as colourful and decorative as they like – which they bring to the next lesson, with their names at the bottom. The posters are pinned to the wall around the class. Students walk round looking at the posters. If they have any questions or comments, they note the name of the writer and bring up the question/comment in a later full-class discussion.

2   Instead of superordinates, challenge students to find *hyponyms* (specific kinds of the target word). For example, if the word was *bag*, they might find *sleeping bag, handbag, backpack*.

Notes

1   This is a more advanced version of 1.2.5 *How else could you say it?*, which elicits direct synonyms; here students are looking for a wider range of items belonging to the relevant generalized category.

2   Note that verbs are more likely to elicit multi-word phrases as well as single words.

Box 3.2.7: Related words

Nouns	Verbs	Adjectives
• coffee	• advise	• cold
• house	• fly	• delighted
• laptop	• jump	• old
• lake	• pay	• sick
• robbery	• say	• soft
• tree	• send	• quick
• yacht	• smell	

 Teaching tip

More advanced or academically oriented classes may benefit from learning the metalanguage associated with vocabulary learning: *connotation, collocation, hyponym, superordinate, synonym, antonym, formulaic expression, context of use, morpheme, prefix, suffix,* etc.

3.2.8 Connotations

Outline	Students identify connotations of particular items.
Focus	Exploring connotative meaning (associations, positive/negative implications, etc.)
Age	Adolescent–Adult
Level	Advanced
Time	Five minutes in the first lesson, 20–30 in the next
Preparation	*Box 3.2.8*, copied for students

Procedure

1 Explain the word *connotation* as distinct from *denotation* (simple meaning or reference). Give the example of the word *dog*: ask students what connotations this word has for them. Some may suggest inferiority (as, for example, in the idiom *a dog's life*), others faithfulness (*a man's best friend*). Ask students if there is a difference between the connotations of the equivalent word in their L1 and those of *dog* in English. Ask the same question about the adjective *red*. Its denotation is simply a bright primary colour; but its connotations may involve things like danger, embarrassment or anger. Again check if it is the same in the students' L1.
2 Tell students for homework to select three words from the categories listed in *Box 3.2.8* and find out what connotations they have in English – from their own intuitions, or from informants who are highly competent speakers of English. Dictionaries may or may not help!
3 Share ideas in full class in the following lesson.

Variation

With a monolingual class you might suggest that they look at the L1 translation of each word they study in this way. Does the English word have similar connotations to the word in students L1? Different? In a multilingual class, students might tell each other about the connotations of the equivalents in their own languages.

Notes

1 This is a 'one-off' activity, designed to raise awareness, so that in future vocabulary learning students will be more conscious of the need to find out connotations as well as denotations of new items.
2 See also 3.2.1 *It doesn't mean quite the same thing (1)*.

Box 3.2.8: Connotations

1 materials (iron, steel, plastic ...)
2 colours
3 light and dark
4 parts of the body or face
5 flavours
6 textures (soft, rough ...)
7 human biological or social roles (mother ...)
8 movement
9 speech

From *Vocabulary Activities* © Cambridge University Press 2012   PHOTOCOPIABLE

3.2.9 Is it appropriate?

Outline	Students analyse a particular text for appropriate/inappropriate items.
Focus	Appropriate choice of items in context
Age	Adolescent–Adult
Level	Advanced
Time	20 minutes
Preparation	A text from a specific discourse genre (an email, for example, or a newspaper report), copied for students; use one of the texts shown in *Boxes 3.2.9a* and *b*, copied or displayed for students, or your own text.

Procedure

1 Give students time to read the text and make sure it is all understood.
2 Ask them to underline any items in the text that seem to them particularly typical of, or appropriate to, this genre, and which would be less likely to be used in another context.
3 Elicit and write up these items on the board. Add any more that you would suggest yourself.
4 Discuss with students which other, more neutral, items could have replaced these in a different context. For example, we would probably say *because* rather than *inasmuch as* (business letter, line 13); *badly* rather than *rotten* (blog, line 4).

Variations

1 Present two completely different texts together (such as the two shown in *Boxes 3.2.9a* and *b*) and invite students to compare their vocabulary, rather than analyzing each on its own.
2 After teaching the new vocabulary from any text in your coursebook that is of a specific genre, spend a few minutes discussing the vocabulary from the point of view of appropriateness. Relatively neutral genres, such as narrative, general-interest articles and so on will not be so useful for this; choose ones that are more 'special': some examples are listed under *Box 3.2.9c*.
3 Spend a little time talking about slang terms students know: list all the ones you and they know on the board (but be careful of 'taboo' ones: it is possible to include them in some classes and not in others!). Discuss where these would be appropriate and where not.

4 See also *1.2.9 Abbreviated txt* for abbreviations appropriate for emails,
   SMS texting and internet chat.

Note
You'll find that the main criterion of appropriateness is the level of formality;
and it is, perhaps, the most important one for your students to grasp.
Others, however, will also come up: professional jargon, 'teen' language,
modes of address to different kinds of people, language from a particular
speech community (for example, American vs British English), specific
components of texts (like the salutation and valediction of a letter, headlines
of newspapers).

Box 3.2.9a: Is it appropriate?

Text 1: Business letter

Dear Ms Smith,

¹ Over the years we have had to formulate various company
  policies. These policies have never been arbitrarily
  adopted, but rather chosen in order to be able to accommodate our customers by providing our product at the
⁵ lowest conceivable price while remaining in business.

  One of these policies is that our customers have 14 days
  in which to return any merchandise for a full refund. We
  feel this allows sufficient time to inspect our product
⁹ and be assured of its quality.

  We are grateful for the business you have seen fit to
  give our firm and we are proud to have you as one of our
  customers. We cannot, however, authorize the return of
  our merchandise as you have requested, inasmuch as you
¹⁴ took delivery over 14 days ago.

  We regret that we cannot accommodate you in this matter
  and hope you will understand why we must take this
¹⁷ position.

Sincerely,

John Brown

Adapted from http://www.4hb.com/letters/ltrnoreturn.html

Box 3.2.9b

Text 2: Teenage blog

1 ... Anyways, I went to my grandparents' house yesterday. They just came home last month ... During the winter, they make like birds and fly to Texas. Anyways, when I was younger (11 and 12), I used to treat them really rotten. Mostly because they treat me like I was around the age of
5 seven, and maybe I thought that actually being nice to your grandparents wasn't cool. But yesterday I made more of an effort to actually be sweet. After all ... the amount of stuff they've bought me is insane, and they love toting me around and hanging out with me. After all, I am the only young girl they have to do things for! So, from now on,
10 I think I'll try and be a little bit nicer to them, which may not come easy, but I'll try my hardest!

Adapted from http://sillyteengirl.wordpress.com

From *Vocabulary Activities* © Cambridge University Press 2012   PHOTOCOPIABLE

Box 3.2.9c: Is it appropriate?

A selection of discourse genres which are likely to display typical vocabulary

- academic paper
- business letter
- commercial advertisement
- formal greetings card
- informal conversation

- instruction manual
- internet chat, blog
- formal announcement (spoken)
- legal contract
- poetry

3.2.10 Local Englishes

Outline	Students identify English words and expressions that are used only by specific local speech communities. This activity is suitable for very advanced classes.
Focus	Awareness of limitations of local-community vocabulary
Age	Adolescent–Adult
Level	Advanced
Time	30 minutes

Procedure

1 Write on the board the following words:

    1 *billfold*
    2 *fortnight*
    3 *orredy, olledy*
    4 *lakh*
    5 *outwith*
    6 *prepone*
    7 *queue*
    8 *sunnies*
    9 *turnpike*

2 Challenge students to say what they mean, and where they are used. Explain words that they don't know (see *Answers (3.2.10 Local Englishes)*).

3 Tell them that NONE of these items is likely to be understood worldwide, so they aren't very useful in international communication. What do they think would be the more universally understood equivalents?

4 Ask them to suggest words and expressions that are used by people using English within the community where the present class is taking place, but probably not outside it. A lot of these may actually be words from the local language, but typically used by people speaking English within the community; others may be literal translations of local words.

5 Students compile a poster of 'local' English words and expressions, side by side with their international equivalents.

Answers (3.2.10 Local Englishes)

1 *billfold*: American English, meaning a wallet in which you can keep paper money

2 *fortnight*: British (+ South African, Australian, New Zealand) English, meaning 'two weeks'

3 *orredy, olledy*: Singaporean English meaning not only 'already' but also 'at once' ('I must leave orredy')

4 *lakh*: Indian English, meaning '100,000'

5 *outwith*: Scottish English, meaning 'outside'

6 *prepone*: Indian English, meaning 'bring forward the time of' (opposite of postpone)

7 *queue*: British (+ South African, Australian, New Zealand) English, meaning 'line of people waiting for something'

8 *sunnies:* Australian or South African English, meaning 'sunglasses'

9 *turnpike:* American English, meaning 'main road that you have to pay in order to use'

♀ **Teaching tip**

Both teachers and students need to be aware of which vocabulary items are more, or less, useful for international communication. Native-speaker intuitions may not be reliable, as most native speakers use the English of the community they were brought up in, which may include usages limited to that community. It's better to rely on your own intuitive knowledge of what is internationally comprehensible, or check with a 'lingua franca' corpus like *VOICE* (see *References and further reading*).

3.2.11 Compare collocations

Outline	Students in a monolingual class make posters showing word combinations that are different in the L1 and may lead to mistakes.
Focus	Awareness of L1 interference in collocational links
Age	Adolescent–Adult
Level	Intermediate–Advanced
Time	20–30 minutes
Preparation	A few mistakes in English that you have come across based on L1 interference within collocations or multi-word chunks (for example, *make a shower* instead of *have/take a shower*)

Procedure

1 Share with the class mistakes that you have come across or made yourself based on translation of L1 word combinations in multi-word chunks.

2 Ask them if they can add more that they have made themselves in the past or heard others say.

3 Tell them to look through their vocabulary notebooks or lists of words in their coursebook. They should look for more multi-word chunks where different component words would be used in their L1 to convey the same idea. They should underline or highlight any they find.

4 Students get together in small groups to make summaries (small posters) based on their findings, showing the correct English expression clearly written out, and the mistaken (L1-interference-based) expression next to it, crossed out.

3.2.12 Spelling history

Outline	Students learn the historical reason for some odd spellings in English.
Focus	Odd spellings and the reasons for them
Age	Any
Level	Intermediate–Advanced
Time	Two–five minutes
Preparation	Information on the history of the spelling of words in *Box 3.2.12*

Procedure

1 Write up the word *one* on the board, and ask students if they've ever wondered why it's pronounced as if it were spelt *wun*.

2 Tell them that originally the word was pronounced /əʊn/ to rhyme with *bone*: as it still is in other derivatives of the same word: *only* (originally *onely*), *alone, lone, lonely, atonement.*

3 Explain to students that the word was pronounced /wʌn/ in western and south-western dialects of English in the Middle Ages, and this pronunciation gradually became more widespread and displaced the earlier pronunciation, while the original spelling was retained, while less common derivatives (*only*, etc.) retained the original spoken form.

4 Point out that the written form of a word, in principle, is more stable than the spoken; spelling is often retained even when the pronounciation changes: for example, *night* was originally pronounced with a guttural sound before the *t*, as it still is in the German *Nacht*.

5 In later lessons, give them other historical explanations for odd spellings or pronunciations (see *Box 3.2.12*).

Box 3.2.12: Spelling history

one

Originally the word was pronounced /əʊn/ to rhyme with *bone*: as it still is in other derivatives of the same word: *alone, only* (originally *onely*), *atonement, lone, lonely*. The word was pronounced /wʌn/ in western and south-western dialects of English in the Middle Ages, and this pronunciation gradually became more widespread and displaced the earlier pronunciation, while the less common derivatives (*only*, etc.) retained the original spoken form.

busy, bury

A similar development affected the spelling and pronunciation of *busy, bury*: originally pronounced as spelt; but in this case it was the London pronunciation of /bɪziː/ and the Kentish pronunciation of /beriː/ that took over, even though the original western English spelling was retained.

love, son, some

In medieval times, manuscripts were often written in the Carolingian script, which is based on 'minims' or downstrokes, which led to confusion between letters, as can be seen below:

The Carolingian script used the following letters:

ı   for *i*

u   for *u* and *v*

m   for *m*

<minim> results in *mınım*

and <luve> results in *luue*

It was therefore decided to substitute *o* for *u* in common words like *love, son*, and *some* in order to prevent confusion.

For the same reason, an apostrophe was added above the *i* to distinguish it from other letters; this later evolved into a dot.

Continued

Box 3.2.12 (*continued*)

u,v

These were originally the same letter; in medieval documents, they were used interchangeably. The only difference was that if used before a consonant, or at the end of a word, it was pronounced like *u*, and if before a vowel it was pronounced like *v*; So a word written as *euery* was pronounced *every*, *vs* was pronounced *us*, and *you* as it is today.

In order for this letter to be heard as *v* at the end of words like *love, give*, it was therefore necessary to add a vowel: the silent *e*. That's why the *e* in these words does not have the function of lengthening the previous vowel as it does in words like *tone, time*.

w

This is, as its name implies, a double-*u*. It is written more like a double-*v*; but these were originally the same letter anyway. That's why you don't usually get *w* next to either *v* or *u*.

-y/-ie ending to words

Originally, *-ie* was the regular ending to words that are today written with a final *-y*: *countrie, marrie*.

So when the *y* of the present forms of these words transforms into *ie* before a final *s* (for example, *countries, marries*), this actually represents an earlier form of the word.

3.2.13 All you know about a word

Outline	Students prepare PowerPoint® presentations about specific words, drawing together what they have learnt through previous vocabulary activities.
Focus	In-depth study of a word
Age	Adolescent–Adult
Level	Advanced
Time	10 minutes for preliminary explanation; 10 minutes per presentation later
Preparation	Dictionaries, thesauri, grammars, on paper or digital; possibly also corpus-based reference websites as listed under *3.2.6 Literal or metaphorical?*

Procedure

1 Tell students they are to work in pairs researching an English word of their choice.

2 Check which word each pair chooses, in order to make sure that they each choose a different one. Explain to students that their research may include some or all of the following:
   • the word's meaning and connotations;
   • its grammar;
   • contexts in which it is used;
   • collocations and expressions in which it features;
   • its frequency;
   • its synonyms and antonyms;
   • derivatives;
   • etymology.

3 Tell students that they should use dictionaries and thesauri, as well as internet sources.

4 Ask students to prepare PowerPoint® presentations and present these to the rest of the class in later lessons.

> ### ○ Teaching tip
>
> When requiring formal presentations from students, I have found it a good idea to start the ball rolling with a similar presentation of my own. This enables me to model the kind of information, length of presentation and format that I am expecting. It also accords with the principle that you don't ask students to do things you're not willing to do yourself!

3.2.14 German or Latin?

Outline	Students check out the etymology of words.
Focus	Etymology: the source of specific words from Germanic or Latinate roots
Age	Adolescent–Adult
Level	Advanced
Time	15–20 minutes
Preparation	Information about Germanic and Latinate vocabulary in English; see *Box 3.2.14a* copied for students or displayed on the board; possibly lists of abbreviated references to source languages, as shown in *Box 3.2.14b*

Procedure

1 Tell the students some basic facts about the history of the English language (you can see a summary of information in *Box 3.2.14a*).
2 From the information given, ask them to say from which source (Latinate or Germanic) they think the following words derive: *information, flood, deluge, rain, snow, duke, tree, skirt, walk, step, pace, think, meditate.*
3 Encourage students to check their answers with an etymological dictionary or online at the *Online Etymology Dictionary* http://www. etymonline.com/. They might need to know the abbreviations shown in *Box 3.2.14b*.
4 Ask students how many answers they got right.

Variations

1 Instead of the words given here, just ask students to select all the verbs, nouns, adjectives and adverbs in a sentence from a text in their coursebooks, and to guess which of them is Germanic and which Latinate before checking with an etymological dictionary (this would, of course, include grammatical as well as lexical items).
2 Based on the information given in *Box 3.2.14a*, ask students if they would expect a different proportion of Latinate to Germanic words in an academic text from that in an informal conversation. Then suggest that they check it out: choose any sentence they've written down from an informal conversation or email and another sentence taken from a scholarly article, and check out the etymology of the lexical items. They are likely to find a substantially higher proportion of Latinate words in the academic text; though these words will still be the minority of the total words, largely because of the grammatical items, which are Germanic.

Box 3.2.14a: German or Latin?

English is essentially a Germanic language derived from the language of the Germanic peoples (Angles, Saxons, Jutes) who invaded and settled in England during the 5th century AD, supplemented by the Scandinavian language spoken by the Vikings who invaded in the 8th century. The Norman invasion in the 11th century resulted in a huge increase in the number of Latinate words that entered the language via French.

The Germanic words tend to be shorter and denote everyday, basic referents: parts of the body, animals, clothes, natural phenomena, etc. The Latinate words tend to be longer, belong to a more formal register, or denote more abstract concepts, sometimes with implications of aristocracy (compare, for example the Germanic verb *rise* with Latinate *ascend*, or Germanic *house* with Latinate *mansion, villa*).

Later, conquest and trade led to a large number of words being absorbed from other languages: Arabic, Turkish, Dutch, Spanish, Italian, Greek, and others.

English today has a huge lexicon of something like a million words, though a fully competent educated speaker of the language is unlikely to know more than about 60,000 of them.

For more information, see:

Baugh, A. C., & Cable, T. (2002). *A history of the English language* (5th ed.). London & New York: Prentice Hall.

McCrum, R., Cran, W., & McNeil, R. (2002) *The story of English*. Harmondsworth: Penguin.

Box 3.2.14b: German or Latin?
Some common etymological abbreviations

Latinate	Germanic	Other
L. = Latin	O.E. = Old English	Sem = Semitic
M.L. = Mediaeval Latin	M.E. = Middle English	I.E. = Indo-European
Fr = French	O.N. = Old Norse	
O. Fr = Old French	Ger = German	
M. Fr = Middle French	(P.)Gmc = (Proto) Germanic	
Gk = Greek (usually entered English via Latin, considered Latinate)	Goth = Gothic	
	O.S. = Old Saxon	

3.2.15 What did this word mean before?

Outline	Students trace back interesting developments in the meaning of selected words.
Focus	Changes in word meanings over time
Age	Adolescent–Adult
Level	Advanced
Time	Five minutes in the first lesson, 15–20 minutes in the next
Preparation	*Box 3.2.15* displayed on the board or copied for students

Procedure

1 Ask students if they know where the word *language* comes from. They may know it is associated with the French *langue* and means 'a tongue'. Point out that many words for general categories or abstract concepts today were derived from words denoting real-world objects or physical actions.

2 Ask them if they can think of any similar examples, in their own language or in English.

3 Tell them for homework to find out the original meanings of as many as they can of the items shown in *Box 3.2.15*. It's best to check this out in an etymological dictionary, or at the website *Online Etymology Dictionary* http://www.etymonline.com/.

4 In the next lesson, students share and compare their findings.

Box 3.2.15: What did this word mean before?

1 alcohol	11 hazard ....
2 assassin	12 hysterical ....
3 avatar	13 jubilee ....
4 chess	14 malaria ....
5 chocolate	15 melancholy ....
6 complication	16 panic ....
7 cute	17 queen ....
8 enthusiasm	18 salary ....
9 fond	19 silly ....
10 governor	20 villain ....

From *Vocabulary Activities* © Cambridge University Press 2012   PHOTOCOPIABLE

3.2.16 New vocabulary

Outline	Students learn about coinages and invent new English words or expressions.
Focus	New words and the different ways they are coined
Age	Adolescent–Adult
Level	Advanced
Time	30 minutes
Preparation	*Box 3.2.16* copied for students; also *Box 1.4.3* and *Box 1.4.5*

Procedure

1 Tell students that although the basic grammar and lexis of English are fairly stable, an enormous number of words are added to the language every year: to denote new inventions, discoveries and cultural phenomena, for example, or to express new theoretical or ideological concepts and to provide more vivid ways of expressing ourselves.

2 Talk the students through the various main mechanisms through which the language enriches its lexicon, as shown in *Box 3.2.16*. Encourage them to compare these with similar coinages in their mother tongues.

3 In pairs, students try to invent new words, based on one of the mechanisms shown in *Box 3.2.16*.

4 Each pair of students prepares a sheet of paper for each new word they've invented, giving its meaning and explaining how they invented it. As they finish, they post the paper on the board or on the classroom wall, and start another.

5 When there is a fair number of papers posted, or if you see that students have had enough, bring the activity to a close, and invite them to look at each other's coinages.

Follow-up

You may wish in a later lesson to spend a few minutes talking about lexical items that go out of use for various reasons: because the items they denote are no longer used (*hansom cab, crinoline*) or because they have been replaced by different words for no obvious reason (*backpack* for *rucksack, vocalist* for *singer*), or because of pejorative implications (*disabled person* for *cripple, senior citizen* for *old man/woman*), or because their use as relating to aspects of sex have made it difficult to use them in their original sense (*gay, intercourse*).

Variation

If you don't want your students to invent new words, simply ask them to find and add at least one item to each of the categories shown in *Box 3.2.16.*

Note

Some of the words they 'invent' may in fact exist: tell them to check them out on a web browser!

 Teaching tip

It may seem rather pointless to invent words that as far as the students know don't exist, but this exercise is a good one for raising awareness of how new words evolve, and to make it therefore easier for students to recognize and identify the meaning of similar coinages when they come across them in texts. It also raises awareness of morphology, and can be used when students are learning about prefixes and suffixes.

Box 3.2.16: New vocabulary

Mechanisms by which the language coins new words

Affixation (prefixes and suffixes)

- disinformation
- understandable
- outsource
- megabucks
- downsize
- upmarket

Borrowing

- déjà vu
- kibbutz
- yoghurt

Loan translation (calque) (the new item is a literal translation of an expression in another language)

- superman
- world view
- brainwashing

Eponymy: (words based on names: brand names, names of people, mythological references, places)

- hoover
- sandwich
- a babel of voices
- kleenex
- herculean task

Blending (the beginning of one word with the ending of another)

- pictionary
- brunch
- chocaholic

Initials (each letter said separately)

- e.g
- UN
- i.e.
- BBC

Acronyms (initials, pronounced as if they were a word)

- radar
- scuba
- NATO
- AIDS

Clipping (shortening)

- bus
- fridge
- movie
- pub
- cute

Continued

Box 3.2.16 (*continued*)

Compounding

- snowshoe
- housewarming
- anchorman

Functional shift (from one part of speech to another; for example, noun to verb)

- impact (noun to verb)
- produce (verb to noun)
- pioneer (noun to verb)
- right (adjective to adverb)

Onomatopeia (the imagined sound)

- cackle
- growl
- murmur
- bang
- ring
- click

Meaning shift or extension

- mouse
- paste
- search engine
- (web)site

Euphemism (a softer or more delicate reference to something possibly embarrassing or offensive)

- bathroom
- restroom
- pass away
- make love

Coinage (totally new invented words)

- googol
- blurb
- cyber

Phrasal verbs

- copy in
- send up
- take over
- take on

Fixed phrases

- couch potato
- spotted kingfisher
- chief of staff

4 Vocabulary testing

Here are some types of vocabulary testing items you might like to use, with notes on variations and associated advantages and disadvantages. In contrast to the activities shown in previous sections which promote vocabulary learning and motivation, the design of these items prioritizes accurate assessment of aspects of vocabulary knowledge, together with convenience and accuracy of marking and grading.

Also in contrast to previous sections, the first heading in many of the activities is *Design*, which includes any necessary preparation, rather than *Procedure*, since it is the design and preparation of the test items which demand the most care and attention rather than how you administer them in class. Time is not normally defined, since this would obviously depend on how many items you include in the test paper.

See *Guidelines* for some general information and tips on vocabulary assessment.

4.1 WRITTEN TESTS

Most language tests are written, since these are most convenient and cheap to administer, and easiest to assess. The procedure, unless otherwise noted, is fairly standard: start by explaining the format and grading system, give out the test sheets, allow time to complete them, take them in and mark them!

4.1.1 Multiple choice

Outline	Students choose the right answer out of a choice of four options.
Focus	Receptive knowledge of the meaning of a written item
Age	Pre-adolescent–Adult
Level	Any

Design

1   Select the vocabulary item you want to test, and prepare for it four plausible definitions or synonyms of which only one is right:

> A customer is ...
>
> a) a counsellor   c) someone who buys   d) someone who sells
> e) someone who keeps to routines.

2   Alternatively, do it the other way round: have the definition as the 'stem', and the right answer as one of the 'options':

> Someone who buys goods or services is a ...
>
> a) servant   b) salesperson   c) dependent   d) customer.

Procedure

Students circle or underline the right answer in each case.

Variations

1   Instead of definitions or synonyms, there are various other kinds of 'stems' you can use:

>   1   Examples:
>   An example of a container is
>   a) a basket   b) a knife   c) a telescope   e) a book.
>   2   Antonyms:
>   The opposite of *heat* is
>   a) cool   b) melt   c) combine   e) warm.

3   Sentence completion (particularly useful for testing collocations):
    He trembled with . . .
    a) fear   b) boredom   c) tiredness   d) sadness.

4   Translation (either way: the 'stem' in L1 and the options in
    English, or the other way round)

5   Two correct answers:
    Something you use to write with is
    a) a pen   b) a picture   c) a book   d) a pencil.

6   Three correct answers:
    You can . . . money.
    a) spend   b) waste   c) eat   d) save

2   To make the items a little easier (both for student and for teacher/
    composer!), have only three options instead of the conventional four.

Notes

1   There is an element of chance: learners have a 25% chance of landing on
    the right answer even if they choose random responses, and may choose
    the right option by process of elimination, rather than by knowing what
    the correct answer is.

2   Multiple-choice items are very quick to answer and easy to check and
    grade. This is why they are the basis for many computer-based tests: they
    can be graded in moments by the computer, with no teacher intervention.
    They are, however, time consuming and tricky to create. Each item takes
    several minutes to compose, and only a few seconds for the students
    to do. And it's quite difficult to compose items that do in fact assess
    knowledge accurately. Make sure that:
    • only one option (if that is what you intend) is the right one; very often
      more than one could be right;
    • the right option isn't the longest one: novice test-writers tend to make
      the right answer also the longest, in an attempt to make sure that this
      is absolutely accurate;
    • only vocabulary that students know is used in distractors.

> ○ **Teaching tip**
>
> Tell your students that they should always fill in an answer to a multiple-
> choice question, even if they don't know the right answer. They should try
> to eliminate first any they are sure that are wrong, and then guess one of the
> remaining options.

4.1.2 Gapfills

Outline	Students fill in a gap in a given sentence.
Focus	Productive (or receptive, as in the *Variations*) knowledge of the written forms and meanings of items
Age	Pre-adolescent–Adult
Level	Any

Design

1 Write a series of ten sentences, each of which clearly contextualizes one of the items you want to test.
2 Delete the item and insert a space where it would have occurred in the sentence, making sure that there is enough room for the students to write it in. For example, if the target item is *delicious* you might write something like:

> I enjoyed that salad very much; it was absolutely ....

Procedure

Students fill in the gaps in each sentence.

Variations

1 To make it easier, write in the first letter of each word on the test sheet:

> I enjoyed that salad very much; it was absolutely d ....

2 Another way of making this test easier is to provide a 'bank' of the missing items, so all the students need to do is identify and copy them in the right context:

> (a picture, tea, a book, bread)
> a   We can drink ....
> b   We can eat ....
> c   You can read ....
> d   You can look at ....

3 Or we can provide three or four options (*multiple choice*) for each item:

> a   We can drink .... (tea, bread, pasta, meat)
> b   We can eat .... (a table, ice cream, coffee, water)

4 Slightly more difficult is to provide a *bank* of items, only some of which are in fact right. This can also be presented in a *matching* format (see *4.1.3 One-to-one matching*):

> a   A horoscope tells you about your   i   independence
> b   If you talk very softly, you talk in a   ii   congress

c	I'm very busy; I have a lot on my	iii	heel
		iv	voice
d	This elegant shoe has a very high	v	whisper
e	In 1984 India achieved	vi	future
		vii	mind

But note that in *Variations 2, 3* and *4* the test will only check receptive, not productive, knowledge of the items.

5 Another possibility is to provide a simple *base* form of a word, and ask the students to insert the correct form; for example:

The young pianist showed great.......................... . (able)

Notes

1 Gapfills are easier to design than multiple-choice items, and almost as easy to mark. They may not, however, in practice target the items you intended! What do you do if a student fills the gap in step 2 of *Design* with another word which makes equal sense in the context: *marvellous, yummy, scrumptious, lovely* . . .? This, of course, can be avoided if you go for the *Variations* above; but if you don't, then you will probably have to accept any reasonable 'filler'! (However, in my experience, students are usually aware of which words you are trying to test, and will use the ones you expect.)

2 When you are marking, I suggest allowing two points for each item; allot one if the student obviously knows and could say the right word even if the spelling is wrong; and the second if the spelling is also correct. (This would not apply to variations where the spelling is provided.)

⏻ **Teaching tip**

Make sure that your students know in advance how the points will be allotted for each item. Provide this information when giving out the tests, and make sure it also appears on the test sheet itself.

4.1.3 One-to-one matching

Outline	Students indicate matching items in two columns of words and their definitions.
Focus	Receptive knowledge of the meaning of the written form of items
Age	Adolescent–Adult
Level	Any

Design

1 List the words you want to test in a vertical column. In a parallel column list their definitions, but in a different order. For example:

1 medicine	a a person you go to see if you feel ill
2 doctor	b when you feel unwell, you may have this
3 hospital	c where you lie and rest when you are ill
4 bandage	d something you drink to make you feel better
5 illness	e something you put on a cut to stop the bleeding
6 bed	f a place where people go to get medical treatment

2 Number the left-hand column with numbers and the right-hand column with letters.

Procedure

Make it clear in your instructions how students are to match the items. One possibility is drawing lines to join the matching items; but this can sometimes produce a confusing criss-cross of lines which is very difficult to untangle for assessment purposes later. It is usually better to write out the numbers below, with a space by each and then tell students to fill in the appropriate letter by each number. Alternatively, add a space for a letter at the end of each numbered item and tell students to fill in the letter.

Variations

1 Instead of words and their definitions, there are a number of other types of 'matches' you might use:
   • pairs of antonyms (*large + small*) as in *Box 4.1.3a*
   • pairs of synonyms (e.g *large + big*) as in *Box 4.1.3b*
   • paired expressions (*to and fro, more or less*) as in *Box 4.1.3b*

- words that collocate with one another (*work + hard*)
- beginnings and endings of idioms, proverbs, cliches, etc. (*No news is + good news*)
- items and their L1 translations (for monolingual classes)
- word components (such as prefixes, suffixes or other morphemes (*micro + phone*).

2 Instead of the conventional two columns, there are other formats you might consider: see in *Boxes 4.1.3a–d*. In order to make this activity slightly more difficult, and to lower the likelihood that students choose the right matches by chance, insert a few items in one of the columns that have no 'matches' and function as 'distractors'. That way there is no way students can get at a right answer simply by a process of elimination.

Box 4.1.3a: One-to-one matching: horizontal lines

Draw lines to connect opposites.

1 distant	2 bright	3 simple	4 airy	5 orderly	6 bold	7 transparent
a opaque	b stuffy	c timid	d close	e complex	f chaotic	g dim

Box 4.1.3b: One-to-one matching: three columns

Draw lines to connect synonyms.

1 beautiful	a huge	i noiseless
2 quiet	b the same	ii handsome
3 gigantic	c silent	iii alike
4 similar	d lovely	iv colossal

Draw lines to connect the paired expressions.

1 to		a away
2 back	and	b fro
3 for		c forth
4 far		d against

Box 4.1.3c: One-to-one matching: circles

Draw lines to connect the pictures to the words.

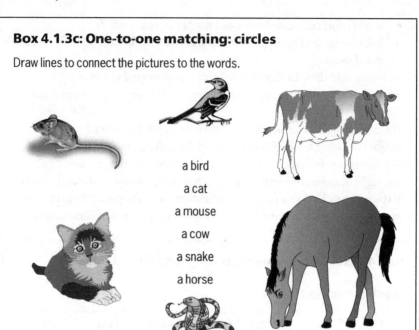

a bird

a cat

a mouse

a cow

a snake

a horse

Box 4.1.3d: One-to-one matching: scatter

Draw lines to connect the nouns to the correct colour.

sky

                 blue   leaves

      red

                                     yellow

banana   green   tomato

Teaching tip

Tell your students in advance how much time they have to do the test, and then let them know when they are halfway through their time, three-quarters the way through, and when they have only ten minutes left. Whether you allow extra time at the end is up to you, or may be laid down by the rules of the institution where you teach.

4.1.4 Multiple matching

Outline	Students match one or two items to several possible corresponding ones.
Focus	Receptive knowledge of meanings of written items
Age	Any
Level	Any

Design

1 Select a number of items you want to test, and list them in a column on the right hand side of the page.
2 Select a criterion which applies to some of the items but not to others, and write it on the left, halfway down the column. For example:

	dangerous
	delighted
positive	shocked
	ugly
	attractive
	brave

Or, for younger beginners

	a horse
	an elephant
big	a mouse
	a cow
	a spider

3 See *Box 4.1.4* for some different ideas for types of multiple matches.

Procedure

Students link the item on the left to those items on the right to which it applies. In this case, the easiest way to do so is to draw lines, as there is no danger of 'criss-cross' confusion.

Variations

1 You can put two items on the left, and make sure that all the items on the right belong either to one or to the other. For example, add *negative* to *positive* in the example above; or see the second item (*make/do*) in *Box 4.1.4*. There will, in this case, be a bit of a 'criss-cross', but it will still be fairly easy to check.

2   To save space on the page, this type of item can be laid out in a linear format: the key item first, and then the set of possible matches beneath, running across the line like a multiple choice; thus:

positive

dangerous   delighted   shocked   ugly   attractive   brave

You can, if you wish, ask students to circle or underline the correct answers instead of drawing lines. The items can be numbered, or lettered, and then students can circle only the number/letter.

Notes

1   This kind of test takes a little time to compose, but is fairly quick later to check and mark. For the marking, allot the same number of points as the items on the right-hand side: for each correct link or not-link, the student gets one point.
2   As with most objective testing procedures there is an element of chance: even a random linking of items from left to right will probably get a few right answers! But if a student gets all of them right, you can be fairly sure they know the target items.
3   This kind of test is more interesting to do than conventional matching test items.

Box 4.1.4: Multiple matching

Use as the criterion for matching one of the following:

* a category or superordinate: *furniture, professions, colours, qualities, abstract nouns.*

	a bed
	a pencil
furniture	a chair
	a window
	a book

* collocates: a verb, with a selection of possible, or impossible, objects

	a cake
	your homework
make	a mistake
do	your best
	the work
	a decision

* or the reverse: an object with a variety of verbs which could or could not govern it; an adjective, with nouns it could or could not modify; a noun, with adjectives that could or could not apply to it; and so on.
* An item with other concepts which are or are not clearly related to it.

	crime
	housework
the police	detective
	law
	soap
	uniform

4.1.5 Dictation-based tests

Outline	Students write down the target items from dictation.
Focus	Semi-productive knowledge of the written form of the target items
Age	Pre-adolescent–Adult
Level	Any
Preparation	A list of the items you want to test ready to read out

Procedure

Read out the items and tell students to write them down.

Variations

1   For a monolingual class whose language you know, tell students also to write down the L1 translation; then when marking give one point for the correct spelling of each item, and a second point for an acceptable translation.

2   Read out short phrases or sentences that contextualize the target items. For example:

Red is a bright colour.

3   Make sure the students know whether you want them to write out the whole phrase/sentence, or just the target item (*bright*).

4   Provide multiple-choice options for each item, written out on the test sheet that has been distributed to students. So instead of writing out the word, the student simply has to choose the correct option as they hear it. This kind of dictation, of course, tests only receptive knowledge, and is more difficult to compose.

 Teaching tip

Note the differences between *4.1.5 Dictation-based tests* and *2.1.4 Single-word dictation*. Often we use can use the same basic procedure for teaching or testing: the difference is that in teaching we are focusing mainly on consolidating and improving knowledge, whereas in testing we are focusing on assessment of that knowledge. It's important for students to know what the aim of a given activity is; so make sure when you introduce the test version that they know their answers will be checked and graded.

4.1.6 Sentence completion

Outline	Students complete sentences from initial phrases that include the item to be tested.
Focus	Receptive knowledge of the meaning of written items
Age	Pre-adolescent–Adult
Level	Intermediate–Advanced

Design

1 Write the beginnings of sentences, leaving the endings open.
2 Each beginning should include one of the target items, but should not give substantial hints as to its meaning.
3 Indicate the target word by underlining, italicizing or emboldening. An example of a sentence beginning for the word *storm* might be something as simple as:

>   The storm was . . . .

>   But not:

>   A storm was forecast . . .

>   . . . since if students know that *forecast* normally relates to the weather, this would narrow the options for the meaning of *storm*.

Procedure

Tell students to complete the sentences in such a way that the meaning of the target word is clear. For example, to finish the first sentence with the words *very bad* may make sense, but it doesn't show understanding. In order to show understanding, the learner would need to write something like . . . *very bad: many trees were blown down* or . . . *the cause of severe flooding.*

Variation
Use sentence endings instead of, or as well as, sentence beginnings. For example:

>   . . . . because of the storm.

Notes

1   This format is easier to design than multiple choice or gapfills; but it is also more difficult and time consuming to mark. The decision as to whether a sentence ending demonstrates understanding of the item or not is, to some extent, subjective.

2   Then there is the question whether to deduct points if there are grammar or spelling mistakes in the sentence ending. Again, I would suggest crediting the student with one point if their sentence clearly shows understanding of the target item, and a second if they have also produced a correct sentence.

3   Another point to bear in mind is that this technique challenges students to use their own originality and creativity: it is therefore a lot more interesting to do.

♀ Teaching tip

It's always a good idea to provide at the beginning of each section of a written test not only the instructions but also one answer filled in as an example. This, of course, will not count towards the test score, but gives the students a clear idea of what is expected.

4.1.7 Cloze[1]

Outline	Student fill in a gapped text.
Focus	Productive knowledge of target items
Age	Pre-adolescent–Adult
Level	Intermediate–Advanced

Design

1 Write a text that contextualizes the target items, leaving gaps for these items for students to fill in.
2 Make sure that if the item is a multi-word expression you have left a long enough space to fill in all the words; you may wish to have a series of separated 'underlines' to show how many words are needed.

Procedure

Tell students to fill in the gaps with the target items.

Variations

1 If the items were taken from a reading text, you may simply use the reading text itself, with the target items missing. This saves you a lot of work, and is not 'cheating'. If the students can fill in the items correctly, this is reasonably reliable evidence that they know them, even if the context is familiar,: you can only normally recall items in context if you have understood them. This variation has the added advantage of being a built-in review of the text itself.
2 You may wish to provide the target items in a *bank* before or after the text itself. This makes it easier – and eliminates the likelihood of students putting in other words they happen to know that fit the slots – but then it will demonstrate only receptive, not productive, knowledge of the items. Another variation is to provide multiple-choice options at each gap. Again, this makes the test easier and more 'receptive' in nature; but it is much easier to mark and gives more objective results.

Note

This is very like 4.1.2 *Gapfills* but since it requires completion of the items within a full coherent text it is a better test of their use in context.

---

[1] I have used this term because it is well known, even though strictly speaking a 'cloze' test omits words at regular intervals (every seventh word, for example), in order to test general proficiency, grammatical competence and reading comprehension as well as vocabulary. Here, gaps are positioned to target particular items in order to focus on vocabulary.

4.1.8 Write sentences

Outline	Students write sentences contextualizing target items.
Focus	Semi-productive knowledge of the meaning of an item
Age	Adolescent–Adult
Level	Intermediate–Advanced
Preparation	A list of the items you wish to test, copied for students or displayed on the board

Procedure

Simply instruct students to compose a sentence for each word that will show they understand it.

Variations

1   You can ask students to contexualize all the items in a single text: a description, a story, an explanation. This is much more tricky, but perhaps more interesting and challenging.

2   Another possibility is to ask students actually to define the target item, to explain what it means in their own words. This is much more difficult to do, at least in writing, so perhaps suitable mainly for more advanced students (see an easier option in the section on spoken tests below), but will give a clearer idea of how accurately the students understand the meaning of the target item. However, the fact that the students can define a meaning does not necessarily demonstrate that they know how to use the item in context.

Notes

1   Writing sentences gives a clear idea not only of whether the students know the meaning of the item, but also of whether they know how to use it in combination with other items, and how it works grammatically. It is therefore 'semi-productive': the word itself, correctly spelt, is supplied, but students need to know how to use it in their own productive composition of sentences. This type of item is obviously very easy to prepare, but very much more difficult and time consuming to check and grade later.

2   As with *4.1.6 Sentence completion* there is the question of whether to deduct points if there are grammar or spelling mistakes in the sentence ending. Again, I would suggest crediting the student with one point if their sentence clearly shows understanding of the target item, and a second if they have also produced a correct sentence.

4.1.9 Say if you know it (1)

Outline	Students say if they know an item or not.
Focus	Subjective assessment of knowledge of an item
Age	Adolescent–Adult
Level	Any
Preparation	See *Box 4.1.9* for a table which can be completed with items you wish to test, with space beside each item for a student to tick *yes* or *no*

Procedure

Students are asked to complete the table by ticking *yes* or *no* at each item, indicating whether they think they know its meaning.

Notes

1   This type of text was first developed by Paul Meara and his colleagues in the late 1980s (see *References and further reading*). At first glance it looks as if it may not give valid results, since it relies mainly on students' subjective assessment of their own knowledge and on their honesty in representing it. But in fact results of such tests have been found to correlate very highly with those of conventional formal vocabulary tests (see the article by Mochida and Harrington (2006) in *References and further reading*). And it is very easy both to design and to check.

2   It does not, however, check the ability of the students to use the item in context, or how thorough their knowledge of its meaning(s) is. For a more sophisticated development of this type of test which attempts to cover at least the first of these aspects, see *Box 4.1.10* below.

3   The fact that the students are assessing their own knowledge means that this type of test is particularly useful during a course as a means of raising their awareness of what they do and do not know, and what they need to learn. This is true also of *4.1.10 Say if you know it (2)*.

Box 4.1.9: Say if you know it (1)

Do you know these words? Tick (✓) the correct column in the table.

Words	Yes	No
1		
2		
3		
4		
5		
6		
7		
8		
9		
10		

4.1.10 Say if you know it (2)

Outline	Students say how well they know an item; if they know it well, they write a sentence using it.
Focus	Subjective assessment of knowledge of an item, as well as semi-productive knowledge as shown in sentence writing
Age	Adolescent–Adult
Level	Any
Preparation	See *Box 4.1.10* for a table which can be completed with items you wish to test. For each word or expression, students have different options as to how to complete the table, in order to express how well they think they know a vocabulary item.

Procedure

Students are asked to choose between five statements which describe how well they know each of the five items in the table. They then complete the table according to which statement they choose. For example, if they choose statement *e*, they should write a short sentence contextualizing the target item in the table.

Note

This type of test is much more time consuming both to produce and to check than the previous one, but gives a much clearer idea of how well the student knows the item.

Box 4.1.10: Say if you know it (2)

Look at words 1–5 in the table and choose the correct statement a–e.

1   For statements a and b, put a tick (✓) in the correct column of the table.
2   For statements c and d, write a translation or definition of the word.
3   For statement e, write a sentence using the word.

	1	2	3	4	5 ....
a I haven't seen this word before.					
b I have seen this word before, but I don't know what it means.					
c I have seen this word before and I think it means . . .					
d I know this word. It means . . .					
e I can use this word in a sentence.					

From *Vocabulary Activities* © Cambridge University Press 2012   PHOTOCOPIABLE

4.1.11 Translate

Outline	Students translate target items into the L1, and (*Variation 2*) from L1 to the target language.
Focus	Receptive (and productive) knowledge of written form and meaning
Age	Any
Level	Any
Preparation	A list of target words or expressions, with space for writing beside each

Procedure
Ask students to fill in L1 translations. They may offer more than one translation for each item.

Variations
1 Providing a single item without context may be appropriate for beginner level, where students don't have that many items to choose from anyway, but at intermediate and advanced level it may better to provide the item within a sentence context in order to prevent ambiguity, even if all you require is the translation of the target item itself. However, in this case be careful not to give away the meaning by providing a context that makes the meaning of the item too obvious. For example:

    They tore away.

    might be a good context for *tore*, preventing students from writing down the translation of the more conventional meaning of *tear*. However, to write:

    They tore out of the house in terror.

    might give away the answer even if the students don't know this meaning of *tear*.
2 Translating from L1 into the target language is a reliable and convenient way of checking productive knowledge. If you demand the translation of full sentences, you will get a very good idea of how well the students both understand and can use the item in context.

 Teaching tip

A lot of teachers feel uncomfortable and even guilty about using translation. It is, however, no less accurate in its results than any of the other testing methods are convenient to use. Obviously it can only be used if members of your class share the same language, and if you know it yourself: but if these conditions are met, there's no need to feel guilty about it!

4.1.12 What goes with this item?

Outline	Students suggest words that are associated with the target words in different ways.
Focus	Knowledge of a word's meanings, collocations and possible uses
Age	Adolescent–Adult
Level	Intermediate–Advanced

Design

Provide a list of the words or phrases that are to be tested. After each, give room to write in another word or phrase that has a given relationship with the original item: a synonym, an antonym, a collocation, another word from the same word family, another word that belongs to the same lexical set, or at least two different possible meanings (explained, or translated into the L1). For example:

Give at least two possible meanings for the following words:

1 bear...

2 direct...

3 character..

4 faint...

5 mean..

Variations

1 Provide a second line for each item, on which students may write in any comments (in either L1 or L2, depending on their level). For example, they might write that the synonym they gave is more formal, or less formal, than the original.

2 For more advanced classes, request three or more different kinds of associations to be filled in. For example:

a For each of the following items give the information required.
notice
i most common meaning(s) (explained or translated):....................
ii a collocation (another word or words that might follow or precede this word in a sentence):...
iii another less common meaning:..
iv another word from the same word family (for example, with different or added prefix or suffix):...

Notes

1 This kind of test will provide a more complete picture of the depth of knowledge that a student has of the target items, instead of the basic form and meaning which are checked in most conventional vocabulary tests.

2 The 'different meanings' could be, of course, of various kinds: homophones (*bear* (n) the animal and *bear* (v) to tolerate), or metaphorical extensions to a basic concrete notion (*arms* (limbs) and *arms* (guns)), or different parts of speech (*direct* (adj.)/*to direct* (v)).

3 This is a very analytical kind of test, suitable for more academic classes. For more information and ideas, see *Connected words* (Meara(2009)).

○ **Teaching tip**

Make a habit of providing an optional extra section for a test, that students who finish early can go on to do: for example, extra words to write sentences for in *4.1.8 Write sentences*. This keeps them going while other students are still working on the 'core' items, and provides appropriate challenge for the more knowledgeable or faster-working students. To play fair, however, you also need to give them 'bonus' marks (above the standard 100%) to reward them for the extra effort.

4.1.13 Learner lists

Outline	Students decide which items they want to be tested on.
Focus	Lexical items that students select
Age	Adolescent–Adult
Level	Any

Procedure

1 Each student lists ten items (words or expressions) that have been learnt recently and that they wish to be tested on.
2 They give these lists to you as a vertical numbered list, leaving a line space between each item.
3 Write by each item one of the following:

    T (=Translate into L1.) (suitable only for monolingual classes whose language you know)

    M (= Explain the meaning in English.)

    S (=Write a sentence contextualizing this item.)

    C (= Write a collocation – another word or phrase that would co-occur with the chosen item in a sentence.)

4 Explain the meanings of the abbreviations you have chosen to insert.
5 Return the test sheets to the students who composed them, for them to complete and submit for marking.

Variations

1 Step 1 may be done as homework.
2 There are other possible tasks you might add, or substitute, to apply to the items the students choose, for example:

    Syn (=Write a synonym.)

    Ant (=Write an antonym. (opposite))

    A3 (=Write three other words that belong to the same topic area.)

    F2 (=Write two other words that belong to the same word family, i.e. adding prefixes or suffixes or changing the part of speech.)

3 Instead of writing only one task for each item, you might write two or more. For example:

    T, S (=Translate and write a sentence.)

4 Use a list of items you have chosen yourself, rather than ones chosen by the students.

Acknowledgement

This idea was suggested by Paul Nation in *Teaching vocabulary: Strategies and Techniques* (2008). (see *References and further reading*.)

4.1.14 Learner-composed tests

Outline	Students design their own tests.
Focus	Any aspect of vocabulary knowledge, selected by students
Age	Adolescent–Adult
Level	Intermediate–Advanced
Time	30–40 minutes for preparation, not including the test itself
Preparation	A list of 10–20 items you want to test.

Procedure

1 Write on the board, or copy for students, a list of the items you want to test.
2 Put students into pairs or small groups and tell them to compose tests based on these items. They have half an hour (or however long you feel appropriate) to do so. They may do this on computers, if available.
3 At the end of the time, take in the tests they have composed, or tell them to send them to you by email attachment. It doesn't matter if not all groups have got through all the items. Warn them that not all their items will appear in the final test, only a selection.
4 Write out and copy a class test using a combination of items that the students have composed, correcting as necessary. Make sure that there is at least one item from each pair/group.
5 Administer the test in the next lesson.

Note

I have found that using tests based on student composition is likely to lower test anxiety and that these are generally more motivating to do. They also save you work! But check carefully for errors.

4.1.15 Lexical frequency profile

Outline	Students submit written compositions for assessment of overall vocabulary knowledge.
Focus	Level of vocabulary knowledge
Age	Adolescent–Adult
Level	Advanced
Preparation	A piece of original written work from a student; a computer tool that enables you to analyse the frequency of words in a written text: for example, *VocabProfile*: http://www.lextutor.ca/vp/eng/

Procedure

1 Choose a piece of written text composed by the student you are assessing. The composition should not have been written with any particular attention paid to vocabulary, and should be the student's original work.
2 Ask the student to submit the text in digital format.
3 Copy and paste the text into *VocabProfile*. (You will need to discount the proper names in the text: it's easiest simply to delete these before pasting the text into the program.) Clicking *Submit* will immediately give you both the raw numbers and the percentages of words which are up to the first two thousand most frequent words in English ('K2'), as compared to those which are beyond (in the Academic Word List or 'off-list', i.e. less frequent). As a rough guide: a text at advanced level will have about 90% up to K2, 10% beyond; whereas an intermediate text will have about 95% up to K2, 5% beyond.
4 A comparison between a student's earlier and later work in the course should show their progress in overall vocabulary knowledge.

Note

VocabProfile does not make any distinction between *homographs* (for example, *bear* (n) the animal and *bear* (v) to tolerate); or between the different meanings of the same word. Nor does it perceive multi-word expressions as single items. Even so, the results of assessment based on this program have been shown to be valid and reliable (see reference below).

Acknowledgement

The Lexical Frequency Profile was originally devised by Batia Laufer and Paul Nation (see their article in *References and further reading*), but has been extensively used and written about since.

4.2 SPOKEN TESTS

Spoken tests are more time consuming and difficult to administer, since you need to elicit spoken responses in one-to-one interactions, which can take anything from five minutes to an hour. They may also be very expensive if you are paying your testers. But the spoken conversation format allows you to elicit more information about how much the student knows about any particular item, and get a clearer idea of their level of knowledge. Spoken tests are also important for those students who can't read or write very well but may know a lot of vocabulary: such students may not be able to demonstrate their knowledge of vocabulary through a written test.

4.2.1 Read aloud

Outline	Students read aloud vocabulary items and explain them.
Focus	(Receptive) knowledge of the spoken form and meaning of target items.
Age	Any
Level	Beginner
Preparation	A written list of the target items

Procedure

1 Tell the student to read aloud the items you have provided and indicate what they mean: more advanced students can explain, beginners can give examples, point to, mime, or draw the item. If you know their language, translation is also an option.
2 Give them one point for each item correctly pronounced, and one for each correct explanation or translation.

Note
As with dictations, the very fact that a student can say or spell an item correctly is a pretty good indication that they also know its meaning. The following explanation or translation functions mainly as confirmation.

 Teaching tip

When testing students orally, take time at the beginning to give them a couple of items to do as a 'rehearsal', assuring them they won't be graded on them. This familiarizes them with the process and relaxes them.

4.2.2 What's in the picture?

Outline	Students identify the English words for things shown in pictures.
Focus	Productive knowledge of simple items (or receptive as in *Variation 2*)
Age	Young
Level	Beginner
Preparation	Pictures showing the items you want to test

Procedure

1 Give the student ten or twenty pictures, and challenge them to tell you the English word for as many as they can.
2 Allot a point for each picture correctly identified.

Variations

1 You'll find that sometimes the student will say something that is near to the target word, but slightly mispronounced. In this case, give them half a point: it's a fairly clear indication that they know the item at least receptively.
2 An easier variation that tests only receptive knowledge is to display all the pictures, call out a word and challenge the student to pick out the matching picture.

4.2.3 Repeat after me

Outline	Students repeat a sequence of words after the teacher.
Focus	Receptive knowledge of the spoken form (and meaning) of the target items
Age	Young–Adolescent
Level	Beginner–Intermediate
Preparation	A set of meaningful word sequences (short lists, phrases or sentences) of between three and six words, which include the items to be tested.

Procedure

1 Say one of the word sequences clearly twice, at normal speaking speed, and ask the student to repeat it after you. Continue to do the same for the rest of the sequences.

2 Give one point for each sequence that is repeated reasonably correctly.

Variation

If you like, ask the student also to tell you the meaning of the sequence: to translate or explain. But you will find that if they have repeated it correctly, it's likely that they will also know what it means: most people cannot repeat more than a syllable or two that they hear unless they understand it. (Try repeating a sequence of four words that someone says to you in a language you don't know, and you'll see what I mean!)

4.2.4 How well do you know this word?

Outline	Students are interviewed to find out how well they know the target items.
Focus	Accuracy of knowledge of basic meaning and spoken form of target items
Age	Adolescent–Adult
Level	Intermediate–Advanced
Preparation	A list of items that are to be tested

Procedure

1 Say a word or expression to the student, and ask them specific questions in order to find out which of the following responses is appropriate: for example, *Have you come across this word before?* and so on. Or, with more advanced classes, provide the student with the options and ask them which would be appropriate relating to the item they have just heard:

- I haven't come across this word before.
- I have come across this word before, but I don't know what it means.
- I have come across this word before and I think it means ...
- I know this word. It means ...
- I can use this word in a sentence.

2 At the end of the process, the teacher should be able to define the student's knowledge of a particular item according to the following levels:

1 The item is not familiar at all.
2 The item is familiar, but its meaning is not known.
3 The meaning is known; a correct synonym or translation is given.
4 The word is used with semantic appropriateness in a sentence.
5 The word is used with semantic appropriateness and grammatical accuracy in a sentence.

Acknowledgement

This is based on the Vocabulary Knowledge Scale developed by Wesche and Paribakht (see *References and further reading*).

 Teaching tip

In oral tests, present the items to be tested at normal speaking speed, repeat as necessary. Presenting them slowly may distort the pronunciation and may not show if the student could in fact understand them in natural interactions.

4.2.5 What more do you know about this word?

Outline	Students are interviewed to find how rich their knowledge of a word is.
Focus	In-depth knowledge of the meanings and uses of a word
Age	Adolescent–Adult
Level	Intermediate–Advanced
Preparation	A list of words that are to be tested

Procedure

1 Say a word and ask questions to elicit from the student what aspects of it are known. These should include some or all of the following:
   - Meaning, or meanings
   - Pronunciation and spelling
   - Grammatical variants (if any, for example, irregular plurals)
   - Grammatical links: how it is used in a sentence
   - Collocational links: what other words are likely to co-occur with it in a sentence
   - Context of use: where, when and why you might use it
   - Synonyms and antonyms
   - Derivatives: other words based on the same *root* word.

   Questions might include all sorts of informal probing questions to elicit knowledge: *Do you remember where you've come across this word?*; *Can you tell me any more about this word?* and so on.

2 The knowledge of each item is graded as:
   1 Inadequate (can't recognize or use the item)
   2 Adequate (knows the basic form and meaning, but no more)
   3 Good (has some knowledge about additional meanings and use)
   4 Rich (has extensive knowledge of additional meanings, appropriate use in context, derivatives, etc.)

Variation

In order to speed up the process, you might wish in the interview to ask only about a selection of the aspects of vocabulary listed at step 1 above rather than all of them; the answers are likely to give you a good sample of the student's knowledge overall.

5   Mainly for fun

The activities in previous sections focused primarily on the learning, review or assessment of target vocabulary items, often made more interesting by the use of stimulating tasks and game-like procedures. The activities in this section, in contrast, take 'having fun' as their primary aim; the vocabulary learning is a by-product, as it were. They are suitable for use as lighter breaks from routine, or for end-of-the-lesson or end-of-the-week fillers.

5.1 SPELLING GAMES

5.1.1 Words from letters

Outline	Students compete to create as many words as they can from a mixed set of letters.
Focus	Spelling of simple words
Age	Any
Level	Any
Time	15 minutes
Preparation	A selection of letters from *Box 5.1.1*

Procedure

1 Divide students into teams of four: tell them to choose one 'secretary' whose job it is to write down the words.
2 Tell them you are going to write twelve letters on the board, and they will have to find (and get their secretary to write down) as many words of three letters or more as they can in four minutes. They may not use any one letter more than once in a word. They may not start until you say *Go*.
3 Write on the board twelve letters, scattered round the board. Make sure that at least three of these are vowels, and at least five consonants come from the first column of the table of letters shown at *Box 5.1.1*.
4 Say *Go* and after exactly four minutes *Stop*.
5 Invite the first group to call out their words. Any other group who has the same word says so, and all groups who have it (including the group who called it out) tick it off. The second group then does the same, calling out only those words that have not yet been ticked off. And so on, until all groups have participated.
6 The group with the most words that no other group thought of is the winner.

Variations

1 Instead of having the groups call out their words, simply take in the lists, check them yourself, and announce the winners later. This saves a lot of lesson time, but adds work for you!
2 Judge the winners by other criteria:
   • Groups get one point for each correct word, regardless of how many other groups also had it.

- Groups get one point for a three-letter word, two for a four-letter word, three for a five-letter word and so on.

3   Instead of asking each group to read out the lists consecutively, have the secretaries of each group come to the board and simultaneously write up their lists. (This will work only if there are no more than five groups.)

4   Make the task more challenging by having fewer letters: eight or ten. But make sure that at least three of these are vowels, and another three are common consonants from the first column of the table in *Box 5.1.1*.

 Teaching tip

It's good to have time limits, as suggested in several activities in this book, but you may find that the time I've suggested is too long or too short for your class, and you'll need to change it. Alternatively, tell the class to stop when you see most of the groups are finding new ideas very slowly or not at all, even if the time limit hasn't expired.

Box 5.1.1: Words from letters

Letter frequency

Very common letters	Less common letters	Least common letters
A	B	K
E	C	J
I	M	X
L	P	Q
N	F	Z
O	H	
R	V	
S	W	
T	Y	
U		
D		
G		

5.1.2 Short words from a longer one

Outline	Students form short words using the letters of a longer one.
Focus	Spelling of simple words
Age	Any
Level	Any
Time	15 minutes
Preparation	Examples of words from *Box 5.1.2*

Procedure

1 Write up a fairly long word on the board (for some suggestions see *Box 5.1.2*). You might need to explain the meaning of the word to some classes. Ask students to estimate how many short words they think they'll be able to find by using its letters. Write up the number on the board.
2 Tell students they have three minutes to find as many words as they can, using the letters of the long word. Each student works on their own. They may use a letter more than once in a single word only if it occurs more than once in the long word.
3 After three minutes, let them join together in pairs or threes and combine their lists. They continue working for another two minutes.
4 Ask students to read out their words to you: write them as they say them.
5 Check whether students found the number of words they had estimated at the beginning. (In my experience they usually find more!)

Variations

1 More advanced classes can be given relatively short words, of six or seven letters.
2 Use a word you have recently taught as the 'base' word.

Note

The advantage of using a single word rather than a random collection of letters is that single words will naturally include vowels and frequent, as well as infrequent, letters and allow also for repeated letters.

Teaching tip

In a brainstorming exercise (*How many .... can you find?*), it is very useful to invite students to start by estimating how many items they think they'll find. This gives them a goal to aim for, and a pleasant feeling of achievement if they manage to achieve or exceed it. I've found that usually students underestimate the number of items they'll be able find in any given brainstorm, so they are likely to succeed.

Box 5.1.2: Short words from a longer one

Easier

- completely
- everything
- important
- information
- intelligent
- interesting
- particular
- translation

More challenging

- certainly
- hospital
- language
- laughter
- question
- special
- together
- whatever

5.1.3 Beetle hangman

Outline	Students play 'hangman' with words they have learnt.
Focus	Spelling
Age	Young–Adult
Level	Beginner–Intermediate
Time	10–15 minutes
Preparation	Suggestion for drawing of beetle in *Box 5.1.3*

Procedure

1 Choose a word the students know. Write on the board a series of dashes, representing the letters of the word.
2 Students start guessing the letters of the word in open-class interaction. If they get a letter right, write it in place of the appropriate dash. If they get it wrong, add a bit to the drawing of the hanging man or the beetle (see *Box 5.1.3*).
3 If they manage to get the word before you complete the drawing, then they have 'won'; if not, then they have lost. Keep a score: the winner is the one who 'wins' at least three words.

Variation

Forget about scoring: the student who guessed the word is the one to choose a new word and come to the board to write up the dashes and respond to students' guesses. The student who guesses this one is the next to choose a word, and so on.

Notes

1 The hanging man sketch is the conventional one; the beetle is the one I prefer, as it is equally simple and less depressing! The 'beetle' actually gives one more guess than the hanging man, so raises the chances of the guessers succeeding.
2 This game is fun for all concerned, but the actual amount of learning is fairly small, as most of the time is spent guessing letters more or less at random, without engaging with the target word: only in the last few seconds of the game is the target word actually seen or heard.
3 The amount of learning can be improved if the words are ones the students know and need to review, so can guess more quickly and take less time randomly guessing letters. But then it won't take them so many guesses to get there. In this case, you might draw in the body, head, eyes

and antennae of the beetle, or the gallows and rope of the hanging man, and then tell them they have to guess with the remaining six components of the drawing to complete.

💡 Teaching tip

If you are playing a guessing game where the successful guesser is the one to be the challenger (the one who knows the answer and challenges others to guess it) in the next round, then you sometimes run into a situation where the same person guesses correctly twice. In this case I suggest that you make it a rule that the second time a person guesses right, he or she does not become the challenger again, but has the right to choose who does (someone who has not yet had the chance to 'challenge'). This gives recognition and prestige to the successful guesser, while ensuring that as many different students as possible have the opportunity to be challengers.

Box 5.1.3: Beetle hangman

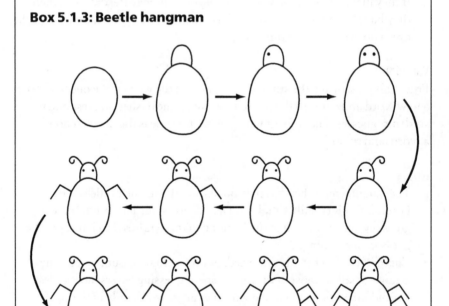

5.1.4 Scrambled words

Outline	Students unscramble words whose letters are in the wrong order.
Focus	Spelling
Age	Young
Level	Beginner–Intermediate
Time	Ten minutes
Preparation	Scrambled words the students know as illustrated in *Box 5.1.4*.

Procedure

1 Write on the board ten or so words that you want to practise, but with the letters in the wrong order, or 'scrambled' in a circle (see *Box 5.1.4*). If they are all the same kind of thing (animals, for example), tell students so.
2 Put students into pairs or small groups, and give them three to five minutes to look at the items and see if they can work any of them out: they are NOT allowed to call out the answers at this point, but they may write them down.
3 Elicit the answers from students. If there are any they can't solve, tell them the answers.

Variation

Transform this into a class-versus-teacher competition; if all the class together can work out all the answers and write them on the board within three minutes, then they have won. If they can't, the teacher has won.

Notes

1 It's easiest to do this by writing out the letters of the word in the same order as you would normally write the word, but simply writing each letter in a different place in a limited space, and then drawing a circle round them. This way you can be sure you remember to write all the letters. If you start writing the letters 'scrambled' (starting with a letter in the middle, then a letter at the end, and so on) you risk forgetting or repeating individual letters.
2 You can, of course, write out the words in linear fashion, making 'nonsense' words, as is conventionally done in quizzes (and shown in the bottom half of *Box 5.1.4*) but it's less easy to guess them, and more difficult to improvise on the board.

Teaching tip

All these kinds of word puzzles (crossword puzzles, wordsearch, scrambles, etc.) are normally based on text written out in upper-case letters. But actually there's no real justification for this other than convention, and beginners can probably decode and understand words a lot more easily if you use lower case. Feel free to use lower-case letters for any word games, as I've done here in 'Scrambled words'.

Box 5.1.4: Scrambled words

Easier: animals

9
b r d
i

10
n
i o
l

More difficult: professions

1 *rngsie* 2 *lodsrie* 3 *nagrame* 4 *turoha* 5 *tolpi* 6 *irverd* 7 *aicncehm* 8 *enegirne*

Answers (Box 5.1.4 Scrambled words)

Easier: animals
1 tiger   2 dog   3 cat   4 mouse   5 horse   6 donkey   7 cow
8 sheep   9 bird   10 lion
More difficult: professions
1 singer   2 soldier   3 manager   4 author   5 pilot   6 driver
7 mechanic   8 engineer

5.2 WORD GAMES

5.2.1 Criss-cross

Outline	Students form criss-cross patterns of words using letter cards.
Focus	Spelling
Age	Any
Level	Any
Time	30–40 minutes
Preparation	*Box 5.2.1a* copied, enlarged and cut up for students; paste onto stiff card, laminate and cut up into single-letter cards; each set is enough for one group of students to play

Procedure

1 Divide the class into groups of three or four, each with one set of letters. Each group sits round a table which has been cleared of all other objects.

2 The letters are placed face down in one corner of the table. Each player takes seven of them at random.

3 The aim is to make a 'criss-cross' of letters, using all the letters available.

4 One player starts, makes a word using as many of their letters as they can – say, *TIME* – and then takes more letters from the 'pool' to bring the number of cards they have up to seven again. The next player adds a word at right angles to the first, building on one of the letters in the first word – say, *TEACH* – again using as many of their letters as possible. The others continue, in turn, building up a 'criss-cross' as shown:

```
            T
    T  H  I  N  G
    E     M     I
 L  A  T  E     R
    C           L
    H
```

5 Players can help each other make words. They may not insert words that do not cross a word already on the table.

6 Dictionaries (digital or print) should be available: one for each group.

7 The game continues until the first group has used all the letters they possibly can and stops playing. The winner is the group which has used most letters (usually the one which finishes first).

8 As the game is being played, go round from group to group. Disqualify any word which is spelt wrongly, or which doesn't exist: that group will have to dismantle or correct the word and any others based on it.

9 After the end of the game, students move around looking at the criss-crosses which have been made by other groups, asking about any words they didn't know.

Note

Students may need to change places at each turn, or swivel the table, so that the player who has to insert a word can look at the words the right way up.

Variations

1 If you have limited time, tell the class they have 20 minutes to play, making as many criss-crossed words as they can. Stop them after 20 minutes; the group with the fewest letters left is the winner.

2 This can be played with the same rules as the well-known game Scrabble ©, though without a board; in that case, use the letter scores shown in *Box 5.2.1b* and tell students to hide their letters (by putting them on a book on their laps, for example). Each student works out how much he or she has scored at each turn, and there are individual rather than group winners.

♀ **Teaching tip**

When using learning games based on sets of cards it is worth pasting the pictures or words onto stiff card and then laminating before cutting up and storing in a plastic envelope. This is time consuming; but then the material can be used lots of times – for years, in my experience! – without getting torn or dirtied.

Box 5.2.1a: Criss-cross

A	E	I	L	N	O	R	S	T	E	U	E
A	E	I	L	N	O	R	S	T	E	U	E
A	E	I	L	N	O	R	S	T	D	U	G
A	E	I	L	N	O	R	S	T	D	U	G
A	E	I	L	N	O	R	S	T	D	U	G
A	E	I	L	N	O	R	S	T	D	U	G
B	C	M	P	F	H	V	W	Y	K		
B	C	M	P	F	H	V	W	Y	K		
B	C	M	P	F	H	V	W	Y	K		
B	C	M	P	F	H	V	W	Y	K		
J	X	Q	Z	J	X	Q	Z	J	X	Q	Z

From *Vocabulary Activities* © Cambridge University Press 2012   PHOTOCOPIABLE

Box 5.2.1b: Criss-cross

A_2	E_2	I_2	L_2	N_2	O_2	R_2	S_2	T_2	E_2	U_2	E_2
A_2	E_2	I_2	L_2	N_2	O_2	R_2	S_2	T_2	E_2	U_2	E_2
A_2	E_2	I_2	L_2	N_2	O_2	R_2	S_2	T_2	D_2	U_2	G_2
A_2	E_2	I_2	L_2	N_2	O_2	R_2	S_2	T_2	D_2	U_2	G_2
A_2	E_2	I_2	L_2	N_2	O_2	R_2	S_2	T_2	D_2	U_2	G_2
A_2	E_2	I_2	L_2	N_2	O_2	R_2	S_2	T_2	D_2	U_2	G_2
B_4	C_4	M_4	P_4	F_4	H_4	V_4	W_4	Y_4	K_4		
B_4	C_4	M_4	P_4	F_4	H_4	V_4	W_4	Y_4	K_4		
B_4	C_4	M_4	P_4	F_4	H_4	V_4	W_4	Y_4	K_4		
B_4	C_4	M_4	P_4	F_4	H_4	V_4	W_4	Y_4	K_4		
J_6	X_6	Q_6	Z_6	J_6	X_6	Q_6	Z_6	J_6	X_6	Q_6	Z_6

5.2.2 Wordsearch

Outline	Students look for words they've recently learnt.
Focus	Review of words previously taught
Age	Young–Adolescent
Level	Beginner–Intermediate
Time	20–30 minutes
Preparation	A wordsearch puzzle, showing at least ten words previously taught, or that you know are familiar to the class, copied for students; you might want to choose words that centre round a particular theme or topic: for example, an upcoming festival. A selection of websites that will construct these puzzles for you can be found at http://puzzles.about.com/od/wordsearches/tp/word-search-makers.htm. Examples of a teacher-made and a computer-made puzzle are shown in *Box 5.2.2*, preceded by the list of 20 target words included.

Procedure

1 Distribute the puzzles and challenge the students to find at least ten words and circle them. They may work in pairs.
2 Students who have found ten words should be asked to write these in a separate list and translate them into L1.
3 Faster-working students can then be asked to find more (see *Note* 2 below).

Variations

1 The puzzles may be made more difficult by increasing the number of words to be found.
2 They may be made easier by providing a list of the target words that can be found, either on the puzzle papers themselves or on the board. Check that these are all understood by the students. If the words are all associated with a particular theme, tell the students in advance what this is.
3 Divide students into groups of three or four, and have a competition: who can find the target words fastest?

Notes

1 Many of the web puzzle-maker programs write your words diagonally, upwards and backwards, as well as left-to-right and downwards: see the example in *Box 5.2.2*. It is, however, preferable to have the target words written only left-to-right and downwards, since the other directions make it rather difficult to identify the words – particularly for learners with reading disabilities – and mean that too much time is spent fruitlessly

searching, rather than actually finding (try the examples given in the *Box*, and you'll see what I mean). The wordsearch maker on the site *Teacherly* on http://freewordsearch.teacherly.com/ avoids this problem, and is very quick and easy to use.

2   All the computer puzzle makers fill in the blank spaces with random letters. But if you fill these in yourself, then you can use them to create more real words. Even if these are as short and simple as *no, and, it,* they provide extra challenge and extra words to find for the faster-working students. See the example in *Box 5.2.2*. So I would recommend creating your own wordsearch puzzles, or to take the one created by *Teacherly* and substitute other letters for the random ones they provide, which will enable students to find more words of their own.

Box 5.2.2: Wordsearch

1   picture
2   computer
3   dog
4   clothes
5   house
6   sun
7   moon
8   bag
9   bottle
10   foot
11   tree
12   flower
13   cup
14   key
15   cat
16   present
17   eyes
18   ball
19   telephone
20   fish

Home-made wordsearch

T	C	U	P	H	E	K	P	E	N
O	L	F	L	O	W	E	R	A	T
P	O	O	C	U	F	Y	E	S	E
I	T	O	A	S	I	T	S	T	Y
C	H	T	T	E	S	O	E	R	E
T	E	L	E	P	H	O	N	E	S
U	S	C	O	M	P	U	T	E	R
R	U	H	B	O	T	T	L	E	F
E	N	A	D	O	G	B	A	L	L
C	A	T	I	N	O	B	O	D	Y

Continued

Box 5.2.2 (*continued*)

Computer-made wordsearch

```
I Y H S H O N Y T F P M D M J
D X Z O C R C E E R T R E X E
R V U F O F L T E K M U F F Y
E S R I M E Z S I L K N G J U
E Y E S P I E N Z B I I K N A
F V W H U N U S C X W C W B D
K G O D T O O F U A L J O Y G
H N L W E O L E B B Q V G H V
E V F X R M L U G F D G N R E
E A R X U T A C W P F W U R N
I E M R T S B T M Q H Z G F Y
E N Y O C I A I H I L S M E Z
B P B K I N G Y X A K F L G H
A V A T P U C S T P E F F R W
Q Q L M D M F Q W Z V U M B Y
```

5.2.3 Crosswords

Outline	Students create and solve crossword puzzles.
Focus	Review of recently taught words
Age	Pre-adolescent–Adolescent
Level	Any
Time	40–50 minutes

Procedure

1 Each pair of students chooses five words they have learnt in this class.
2 Using squared 'arithmetic' paper, the students create a crossword puzzle that has the five words they chose in it, and at least five others which 'criss-cross' with the original words and/or each other. They continue to add words until you say *Stop*.
3 Students then add numbers, so that the first letter of each word, whether vertical or horizontal, has a number, in order of their appearance in the puzzle.
4 They create a clue for each word, in two columns: *across* or *down*. This could be a definition or a translation.
5 They then copy out the blank crossword puzzle and the clues, and give it to you, with their names at the bottom.
6 Your homework is to try to solve the crossword puzzles!

Variations

1 Steps 4 and 5 could be finished for homework, if you run out of time in class. Students exchange their puzzles with each other instead of giving them to you to do, and try to solve each other's puzzles. But it's better to do this as a follow-up (see below) because of possible problems with design or language: designing doable crossword puzzles is more difficult than you might think.
2 Let students use one of the puzzle-maker websites (for example, *Crossword Puzzle Games* http://www.crosswordpuzzlegames.com/create.html) to design their crosswords. This cuts short the time-consuming (but for many students enjoyable) job of design and numbering, and leaves the students free to concentrate on the words themselves and their definitions.

Follow-up

While solving the students' puzzles, note any problems or mistakes and give them back to the students on the following day to correct. Ask them to copy out their corrected versions (blank puzzles and clues) and exchange with other students. They then try to solve each other's puzzles.

5.2.4 Words beginning with ...

Outline	Students brainstorm words beginning with a given letter of the alphabet.
Focus	Review of words previously taught
Age	Young–Adolescent
Level	Beginner–Intermediate
Time	Five–ten minutes
Preparation	Suggested letters and their frequency in *Box 5.2.4*

Procedure

1 Write a letter up on the board (but not *x*!), and tell them we have to find at least 20 words beginning with this letter (or 30 or 40 ... whatever number you think is realistic for your class).
2 Tell them to call out words, and write them up as fast as you can.
3 Note how many you found, and the next time, with another letter, try to beat the class's previous record.

Notes

1 This is a good activity for the end of a lesson when you find you have a few minutes to spare.
2 Use the letter frequency table shown in *Box 5.2.4*. The activity will be easier if you take one of the more common letters as a basis, more difficult if you use the less common ones.

Variations

1 Instead of the first letter, suggest that students think of words that **end** with the letter, or even words that **include** the letter.
2 Supply a set of meaning or word-class categories for which students have to think up at least one item each beginning with the given letter. This can be done in tables, which students can sketch for themselves. See *Box 5.2.4* for some examples.

♀ Teaching tip

A lot of these vocabulary games are good for filling in at the end of a session; they give a pleasant 'rounding-off' feeling. But note that if you spend a lot of time on them during the main part of the lesson this may be at the expense of more substantial language-learning activities, and the more serious classes or students may start getting irritated.

Box 5.2.4: Words beginning with ...

Beginner

Find a word that begins with the given letter, for different kinds of categories.

	A thing	A food	An animal	A name
L	lamp	lemon	lion	Liza
T				
N				

Intermediate

Find a word that begins with the given letter, in different parts of speech.

	Noun	Verb	Adjective	Adverb
L	lamb	like	long	lastly
T				
N				

Find a word that begins with the given letter associated with different topics.

	Sport and games	School and study	House and home	Travel and movement
L	lacrosse	literature	lunch	leap
T				
N				

	A substance or material	A person or profession	An activity	An abstract idea
L	lead	lawyer	laugh	life
T				
N				

5.2.5 Acrostics

Outline	Students make up short texts or poems based on a word written vertically which gives the first letter of each line.
Focus	General vocabulary review
Age	Any
Level	Intermediate–Advanced
Time	20–30 minutes

Procedure

1 Choose a word which students have recently learnt, which has between six and ten letters, and write downwards on the left-hand side of the board.
2 Invite students in open-class interaction to suggest words or phrases that are connected to the meaning of the word. Fill in their suggestions as you get them. For example:

Favourite people

Ready

Interested

Enthusiastic

Near me

Delightful

Stand up for me

3 Now suggest a new word, and tell students to work in pairs to prepare a new acrostic: as before, the list of words and expressions they suggest has to relate in some way to the base word itself.
4 Students read out the resulting acrostics. Even though they all had the same word, the results are often quite different!

Variations

1 Students expand the acrostic words into whole phrases, but keeping the base letters in the middle:

My Favourite people

They are Ready to listen, etc.

2 Students use their own names as bases for acrostics, or the names of their friends.

5.3 PRONUNCIATION GAMES

5.3.1 Tongue twisters

Outline	Students learn by heart and try to say tongue twisters as quickly as they can.
Focus	Pronunciation
Age	Young–Adolescent
Level	Beginner–Intermediate
Preparation	A set of tongue twisters. Use *Box 5.3.1* or find your own.

Procedure

1 Write the tongue twister on the board, and ask students to read it aloud, twice.
2 Erase one word, and ask them to read it again, including the missing word which they have to recall.
3 Continue erasing, until they have learnt the entire tongue twister from memory.
4 Challenge them to say it faster and faster!

Note
This is a good activity for practising difficult pronunciation features.

Box 5.3.1: Tongue twisters

- I scream, you scream, we all scream for ice cream!
- I saw Susie sitting in a shoe-shine shop
- She sells sea shells by the seashore.
- The big fat cat sat on the rat.
- A cup of proper coffee in a copper coffee cup.
- Fresh fried fish, fish fried fresh
- Red leather, yellow leather, red leather, yellow leather.
- Orange jelly, lemon jelly, orange jelly, lemon jelly, orange jelly, lemon jelly.
- Whether the weather is cold, Whether the weather is hot, We'll weather the weather, whatever the weather, Whether we like it or not!
- A big black bug bit the big black bear, but the big black bear bit the big black bug back!
- Four furious friends fought for the phone.
- Green glass globes glow greenly.
- How much wood would a woodchuck chuck if a woodchuck could chuck wood?

5.3.2 Jazz chants

Outline	Students learn by heart and declaim jazz chants in different ways.
Focus	Pronunciation
Age	Young–Adolescent
Level	Beginner
Preparation	A set of jazz chants; use those in *Box 5.3.2* or check out Carolyn Graham's book *Creating Chants and Songs*[1]

Procedure

1   Teach the chant to the class, using claps or finger-clicking to mark the rhythm.

   For example:

   FOOTball, BASketball, GOLF (clap)
   FOOTball, BASketball, GOLF (clap)
   FOOTball, BASketball,
   FOOTball, BASketball,
   FOOTball, BASketball, GOLF (clap)

   (Graham, 2000: 106)

2   Repeat it until the students can easily chant it by heart.
3   Invite them to perform it in different ways: very loudly, very softly; very fast, very slowly; starting softly and getting louder; or the reverse (*crescendo, diminuendo*); in a high or low tone.

Variations

1   Put the class into small groups, and tell them to prepare an artistic rendering of the chant. They may repeat it as many times as they like, use any sound effects and combination of their voices. Then enjoy the performances.
2   Invite students to create a different version of the same chant, using a different set of words.

Acknowledgement

I owe all I know about the use of jazz chants in English teaching to Carolyn Graham.

---

[1] Graham, C. (2006). *Creating Chants and Songs*. Oxford: Oxford University Press.

Box 5.3.2: Jazz chants

1 ZEBra, ELephant, COW (clap)
  ZEBra, ELephant, COW (clap)
  ZEBra, ELephant,
  ZEBra, ELephant,
  ZEBra, ELephant, COW (clap)[1]

2 SUNday, MONday, TUESday, WEDnesday, THURSday, FRIday, SATurday (clap)

3 I like CHOC'late, and I like TEA. I like ICE cream, and I like ME!
  (outside rhythm: Yummy!)

4 I DON'T like BEEtles, and I DON'T like DOGS. I DON'T like MICE and I DON'T like
  FROGS
  (outside rhythm: Yuk!)[2]

5 ONE TWO, I like YOU
  ONE TWO, I like YOU
  ONE TWO THREE, you like ME
  and I LIKE YOU[3]

6 Do you like DANCing? YES, I DO!
  Do you like DANCing? YES, I DO!
  SHE likes DANCing, SHE likes DANCing,
  I like DANCing TOO!

  Do you like TALKing? YES, I DO!
  Do you like TALKing? YES, I DO!
  HE likes TALKing, HE likes TALKing,
  I like TALKing TOO!

  He DOESN'T like JEAN. NO? WHY NOT?
  He DOESN'T like JEAN. NO? WHY NOT?
  He DOESN'T like JEAN beCAUSE she's MEAN,
  But HE likes DOT, A LOT.

  She DOESN'T like BILLY. NO? WHY NOT?
  She DOESN'T like BILLY. NO? WHY NOT?
  She DOESN'T like BILLY beCAUSE he's SILLY,
  But SHE likes DOT, a LOT.[4]

---

[2] Ur, P. (2006). *English 1: Teacher's Guide* (p. 133). Raanana, Israel: Eric Cohen Books.
[3] Graham, C. (1999). *Holiday Jazz Chants*. Oxford: Oxford University Press.
[4] Ur, P. (2007). *English 2*. Raanana, Israel: Eric Cohen Books.

References and further reading

Background, research, theory

Barber, C. (2000). *The English Language,* Cambridge: Cambridge University Press.

Clementson, T., Tilbury, A., Hendra, L.A., Rea, D., Doff, A. & Goldstein, B. (2010). *English Unlimited.* Cambridge: Cambridge University Press.

Chandler, J. (2003). The efficacy of various kinds of error feedback for improvement in the accuracy and fluency of L2 student writing. *Journal of Second Language Writing,* 12(3), 267–296.

Coady, J., & Huckin, T. (1997). *Second Language Vocabulary Acquisition.* New York: Cambridge University Press.

Ellis, R. (2005). Principles of instructed language learning. *System,* 33(2), 209–224.

Laufer, B., & Nation, P. (1995). Vocabulary size and use: lexical richness in L2 written production. *Applied Linguistics,* 16, 307–322.

Laufer, B., & Shmueli, K. (1997). Memorizing new words: does teaching have anything to do with it? *RELC Journal,* 28(1), 89–108.

Laufer, B. (2003). Vocabulary acquisition in a second language: do learners really acquire most vocabulary by reading? Some empirical evidence. *Canadian Modern Language Review,* 59(4), 567–587.

Laufer, B. (2005). Focus on form in second language vocabulary learning. *EUROSLA Yearbook,* 5, 223–250.

Laufer, B., & G. C. Ravenhorst-Kalovski. (2010). Lexical threshold revisited: lexical text coverage, learners' vocabulary size and reading comprehension. *Reading in a Foreign Language,* 22, 15–30.

Long, M.H., & Robinson, P. (1998). Focus on form: Theory, research and practice. In Doughty, C., & Williams, J. (Eds.), *Focus on Form in Classroom Second Language Acquisition* (pp. 15–41). Cambridge: Cambridge University Press.

McCarthy, M., & Schmitt, N. (Eds.) (1997). *Vocabulary: Description, Acquisition and Pedagogy.* Cambridge: Cambridge University Press.

McCarthy, M., O'Keeffe, A., & Walsh, S. (2010) *Vocabulary Matrix: Understanding, Learning, Teaching.* Andover, Hants: Heinle, Cengage Learning.

Meara, P., & Buxton, B. (1987). An alternative to multiple-choice vocabulary tests. *Language Testing*, 4(2), 142–151.

Meara, P. (2009) *Connected Words: Word associations and second language vocabulary acquisition.* Amsterdam, Philadelphia: John Benjamins Publishing Company.

Mochida, K., & Harrington, M. (2006). The Yes/No test as a measure of receptive vocabulary knowledge. *Language Testing*, 23(1), 73–98.

Nation, I. S. P. (2000). *Learning Vocabulary in Another Language.* Cambridge: Cambridge University Press.

Papathanasiou, E. (2009). An investigation of two ways of presenting vocabulary. *ELT Journal*, 63(4), 313–322.

Read, J. (2000). *Assessing Vocabulary.* Cambridge: Cambridge University Press.

Schmitt, N. (2008). Instructed second language vocabulary learning. *Language teaching research*, 12(3), 329–363.

Ur, P. (2009). *Grammar Practice Activities*, Second Edition, Cambridge: Cambridge University Press.

Wesche, M., & Paribakht, T. S. (1996). Assessing second language vocabulary knowledge: depth versus breadth. *Canadian Modern Language Review*, 53(1), 13–40.

Wilkins, D. A. (1972). *Linguistics in Language Teaching.* Massachusetts: MIT Press.

Zahar, R., Cobb, T., & Spada, N. (2001). Acquiring vocabulary through reading: effects of frequency and contextual richness. *Canadian Modern Language Review*, 57(4), 544–72.

Teaching ideas

Gairns, R., & Redman, S. (1986). *Working with Words.* Cambridge: Cambridge University Press.

Goldstein, B. (2008). *Working with Images.* Cambridge: Cambridge University Press.

Graham, C. (2006). *Creating Chants and Songs.* Oxford: Oxford University Press.

Holmes, V. L., & Moulton, M. R. (2001). *Writing Simple Poems: pattern poetry for language acquisition.* Cambridge: Cambridge University Press.

Leaney, C. (2007). *Dictionary Activities.* Cambridge: Cambridge University Press.

Morgan, J., & Rinvolucri, M. (1988) *Dictation: New methods, new possibilities*. Cambridge: Cambridge University Press.

Morgan, J., & Rinvolucri, M. (2004). *Vocabulary*. (2nd Edition). Oxford: Oxford University Press.

Nation, I. S. P. (1994). *New ways in teaching vocabulary*. Alexandria, Virginia: TESOL, Inc.

Nation, I. S. P. (2008). *Teaching Vocabulary: Strategies and Techniques*. Boston: Heinle Cengage Learning.

Schmitt, D., & Schmitt, N. (2005). *Focus on Vocabulary: Mastering the Academic Word List*. New York: Pearson Education.

Thornbury, S. (2002). *How to Teach Vocabulary*. Harlow, Essex: Pearson Longman.

Wajnryb, R. (1990). *Grammar Dictation* Oxford, Oxfordshire: Oxford University Press.

Dictionaries and thesauri

Cambridge Advanced Learner's Dictionary (3rd edition). (2008). Cambridge: Cambridge University Press.

Cambridge Dictionary Online: http://dictionary.cambridge.org/

Longman Language Activator (2nd edition). (2000). Harlow, Essex: Pearson.

Oxford Dictionaries Online: http://oxforddictionaries.com/

The Oxford Dictionary of Proverbs: http://www.oxfordreference.com/

Merriam-Webster Online: http://www.merriam-webster.com/

Roget's thesaurus of English words and phrases (1998).Harmondswoth: Penguin.

Roget's Thesaurus of English words and phrases http://poets.notredame.ac.jp/Roget/

Other useful or interesting websites

American Corpus of Contemporary English: http://www.americancorpus.org/

Babylon: http://www.babylon.com

Behindthename (meanings / etymologies of names): http://www.behindthename.com/

British National Corpus: http://corpus.byu.edu/bnc/

ForBetterEnglish: http://forbetterenglish.com/

JustTheWord: http://193.133.140.102/justTheWord/

Online Etymology Dictionary: http://www.etymonline.com/

The *Lextutor* website, including:
The *LG* site: http://www.lgdtxtr.com/

- Corpus concordance: http://www.lextutor.ca/concordancers/concord_e.html
- Frequency lists: http://www.lextutor.ca/freq/lists_download/
- Vocabulary profilers: http://www.lextutor.ca/vp/bnc/ and http://www.lextutor.ca/vp/eng/

The Phrase Finder: http://www.phrases.org.uk/meanings/proverbs.html
VOICE. (2009). *The Vienna-Oxford International Corpus of English* (version 1.0 online). Director: Barbara Seidlhofer; Researchers: Angelika Breiteneder, Theresa Klimpfinger, Stefan Majewski, Marie-Luise Pitzl: http://www.univie.ac.at/voice/page/index.php

Index

Note: Activity titles are shown **in bold.**

Dictionary Activities
Cindy Leaney

Do you know how to advise your students to get the most out of their dictionary? Do you know what to look for when selecting from the different types of dictionary on the market? Have you ever been disappointed by your dictionary?

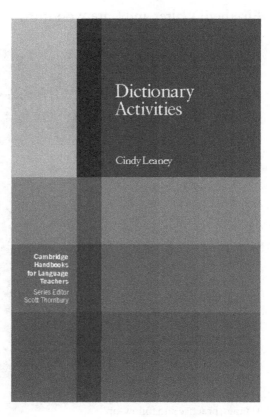

Dictionary Activities will help your students get to know their dictionaries by explaining basics such as what the features of a dictionary are and how to navigate a dictionary, through to more complex topics such as collocations, idioms and word building.
The book also looks at the use of electronic dictionaries and specialized dictionaries such as picture dictionaries.

There are eight chapters which deal with:

- Confidence and dictionary skills-building activities
- Vocabulary-building activities
- Grammar activities
- Pronunciation activities
- Reading and writing activities
- Quick activities
- CD-ROM and electronic dictionary activities
- Specialized dictionaries

In addition to providing over 90 dictionary activities to use in the language classroom, this book will also be invaluable to any teacher who wants to improve their own knowledge of how dictionaries work.

Paperback 978 0 521 69040 9

Collocations Extra

Multi-level activities for natural English

Elizabeth Walter and Kate Woodford

Help your students become natural and fluent English speakers with *Collocations Extra*. Simple to use and quick to prepare, this collection of photocopiable collocation activities encourages students to practise natural language 'chunks' from elementary right through to advanced level. Popular classroom topics and a CD-ROM with templates for games make it simple to integrate these activities into your lessons.

You will like *Collocations Extra* because ...

- over 50 clear step-by-step lesson plans provide you with instant and original supplementary materials to teach collocations.
- input, practice and follow-up stages for each activity introduce students to the collocations and allow them to consolidate their knowledge with a wide range of engaging exercises.
- students can build their confidence and develop natural-sounding English as they practise collocations through a variety of communicative and fun activities including quizzes, board games, questionnaires and picture stories.
- you can create games to practise collocations of your choice using easily adapted templates on the CD-ROM.
- informed by the Cambridge International Corpus, *Collocations Extra* ensures that the most frequently used collocations arepresented and practised in their natural context.

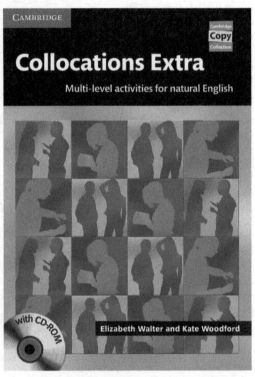

Paperback 978 0 521 74522 2